# Sunshine and Ice

# Volume 8

## Patience and Wisdom

## MARTIN MONEY

First published in Great Britain

All paper used in the printing of this book has been made from wood grown in managed, sustainable forests.

ISBN13: 978-1-78003-777-6

Printed and bound in the UK
Author Essentials Ltd
4 The Courtyard
South Street
Falmer
East Sussex BN1 9PQ

A catalogue record of this book is available from the British Library

Cover design by Jacqueline Abromeit

# PATIENCE AND WISDOM

## March-August 2014

# INTRO – THE RIGHT BALANCE

**There's** a popular saying that you can't please all the people all the time. The older we get, the more we grasp its profound wisdom. It's how we deal with this realization that matters.

Some would add that it's therefore a pointless exercise so we shouldn't beat ourselves up or tie ourselves in knots trying to keep everyone happy at once. I tend to agree.

But I do draw the line at getting overly militant about it. Yes, I'm too long in the tooth to much care what people in general think about me. But those closest? – That's a different matter.

Attempting to please all the people all the time is one thing and it's pretty much doomed to failure. But going to the other extreme and saying "sod 'em all" is also very wrong and will drive people away, leaving you isolated and bitter.

Certainly, your contemporaries should know where you stand on things and you need to show you're confident in your views, values, intentions and abilities, therefore no pushover – for being too malleable and ineffectual can lead to others exploiting and manipulating you, leading to a lot of confusion, frustration and, ultimately, misery.

I'm a great believer that we should be able to stick up for ourselves and not feel intimidated or emotionally blackmailed into doing things just because not doing them might upset others.

Constantly giving in means we end up living our entire lives in accordance with other people's wishes at the expense of our own – maybe even dying full of resentment and regrets. How sad and unnecessary is that?

With regard to the general public and casual acquaintances, if my words and actions infuriate others I'm not unduly concerned.  I've said previously that I spent far too many years trying to fit others' moulds and perceptions, causing me untold grief. Now I'm a lot more confident in myself.

I'm also more assertive, up to a point, with family, dear friends and those closest to me.  The big difference here is that I DO care what they think of me and it matters a great deal when I hurt, disappoint or upset them.

But my new confidence is on a purely personal level.  In practical terms I can be as nervous as hell over certain things - worse than ever. Plus there's a huge difference between confidence and arrogance.  I used to confuse the two – not any more.

For years I thought boxing legend Muhammad Ali was arrogance personified.  I admired his dazzling skills and thought he made the sport interesting with his larger-than life personality.  But I still thought he was an obnoxious big-head.
It took me ages to appreciate that, in fact, what I was seeing was actually supreme confidence in his own amazing abilities. In the ring, he really was the greatest, as he claimed.  A lesser boxer would have had the gob without the goods – arrogance.

I guess at the end of the day we have to steer a middle course between mad self-obsession and a crazy desire to be everyone's friend.

We each have to know when to compromise and negotiate, and when to stand firm to protect our own interests and those of our nearest and dearest.

Of course, to persistently fight your own corner at the expense of your peers is self-indulgence gone bonkers. Life could get very lonely.

Conversely, to always put others first and constantly be at their beck and call puts you in real danger of denying yourself any hope of essential "me time" or personal contentment, satisfaction or happiness.

Genuine friends and properly loving family members would recognise these subtle but vital differences – the self-absorbed and thoughtless would simply get annoyed at your reluctance to constantly indulge them, wondering why you're being so awkward.

The world is full of control freaks and doormats. Some folk are so self-centred and convinced of their own rights and importance that they ruthlessly exploit and manipulate others at every turn, not caring a jot that they have feelings too.

At the other end of the scale are those poor, pathetic souls who have been so ground down by the actions and expectations of others that they have no self-esteem left.

Somewhere between these two extremes lies the right balance of care and consideration for others and sensible self-preservation.

Funny lot, the human race – aren't we?


*****************************************

# CHAPTER ONE – A NEW ERA

**March 2, 2014** – Today's Sunday and I've had a wonderful week.  On Tuesday, February 25 – my 60th birthday - Suzette took me out for a special roast meal and catch-up at a Toby Carvery at Somerford, Christchurch.  Very nice it was, too.

Not only that, my "adopted" sister also gave me a birthday card, W H Smiths gift card, cookies and Mars Bars.  Sweet! (Excuse the pun!).

The following day I went to Boscombe and bought some CDs with my birthday money and two books with the gift card – the 2014 Guinness Book of Records and an anthology of 100 classic poems.

Unfortunately, my sister Carol and hubby David couldn't make it Tuesday – they were otherwise engaged.  But they had put a card containing money in the post – a super, glittery home-made decoupage one emblazoned with the words Happy 60th Birthday Brother.

On Thursday, I was invited to my friends Sam and Carl's house for an impromptu but very enjoyable few hours with them, their little sons Rudy and Bailey, Sam's 17-year-old daughter Rebecca, Albert the terrier dog, and a friend called Jimmy.

Friday evening I was back there, this time for a pre-arranged booze and fun session.

I had been invited a few days previously, but when I turned up I had a nice surprise – our mutual mates Jem Hannen and Tina

Mcauley were already there and they all greeted me with a chorus of "Happy Birthday to You" as I surveyed the cake and buffet they'd laid on for me.

Sam and Tina gave me cards and, a few minutes later, my very good friend of many years Kerry Smith arrived with her son Leon. Kerry had also bought a card from her and her family.

Sam's cousin Jac turned up later – which was cool, as I hadn't seen her for a while. All in all, it was a lovely little party – just right.

Yesterday afternoon, Phil, Emily and Harvey visited me - also armed with cards and a box of chocolates. And, tea-time, I was back at Sam's again. Jac came over from New Milton once more and our pal Sharon Pendleton came along later.

In all, I had nine cards ranging from the stylish to the very funny. My birthday present to myself was a CD of Ellie Goulding's excellent album Halcyon Days.

Continuing the celebration theme, today is Phil and Em's first wedding anniversary. They've gone out for a meal at the hotel they held their reception.

But tomorrow is a sad occasion – it was two years ago that my beloved big sister Jan passed on. I'll light a candle for her and put a little tribute on Facebook.

**March 4** – It's all kicked off in the Ukraine with bitter fighting and dozens of deaths. Russia is poised to invade the Crimean region of its neighbour country and America is warning it not to or face economic sanctions or even military opposition if it does.

The problem seems to have started when President Yanukovych's Ukrainian government rejected a far-reaching accord with the European Union last November in favour of stronger ties with Russia.

Thousands of people, outraged that a long-standing aspiration for integration with Europe had been ditched overnight, poured into central Kiev for peaceful protests.

But as tension grew, violence erupted and the crisis escalated, culminating in Yanukovych's dismissal in a bloody take-over coup.  He fled and is now a fugitive.

Russia apparently sees this as the overthrow of a democratically-elected Ukrainian government – and it's poised to intervene to restore the old regime using military force if deemed necessary.

Britain and other European nations are closely watching the worsening crisis, not too sure what to do.  While keen to help protect the Ukrainians from aggressive invasion, they're just as eager not to upset Russia, which would threaten lucrative trade links.

Already Russian troops on the border have been firing warning shots over the heads of Ukrainian soldiers singing patriotic anthems.

Tough-talking, hawkish American Secretary of State John Kerry is about to fly to the crisis-hit country.  Meanwhile, our own Deputy Prime Minister Nick Clegg has refused to rule out economic sanctions.

The Russian navy is heading for the area as 16,000 of its troops have been put on standby.

Ukraine's Crimean region is one of the main trouble spots,

raising the spectre of another gruesome Crimean War. Nice!

But, as always, this is just one interpretation of the so-called facts as presented to us by our leaders and their media poodles. What is really going on behind the scenes, and why, goodness alone knows!

Except that, in truth, goodness has little to do with it. There are some pretty nasty people out there with cold, calculated, twisted, cruel agendas, driven by a mad impulse to mercilessly exploit others and our planet in the name of self-gratification and greed.

And talking about things not being as they appear, I watched TV coverage of the United Kingdom Independence Party's spring conference in Torquay.

On the face of it, much of what party leader Nigel Farage said about standing up for Britain in Europe, especially over controlling immigration,  made perfect common sense and would have struck a chord with many citizens fed up with our political leaders' consistent failure to grasp the nettle over this contentious issue.

And herein lays a real danger if those citizens decide to vote for UKIP candidates at the next European and local council elections in May.

For I'm really worried that, behind the reasoned arguments and persuasive rhetoric is a right-wing programme that demonizes foreigners and those of different ethnic or religious background. I also suspect an anti-gay element in there somewhere as well.

As if to prove my point, Farage has been forced to defend a stand up comedian who told a series of jokes about foreigners and Muslims at that very conference.

Okay, granted, I've said myself - more than once – that using humour to tackle phobias is good if it makes us see the funny side of absurd fears and prejudices. People can't fight when they're doubled up laughing.

But using cheeky gags and comments poking fun at racism is one thing. In stark contrast, telling offensive jokes viciously attacking those of a different ethnic origin is a totally different ball game.

And I've a funny feeling the comedian at the conference fell into the second category. Not cool!

I also watched TV coverage of the Green Party's spring conference in Liverpool, notably leader Natalie Bennett's keynote speech. Basically, it validated my recent decision to join the Greens by echoing my own views on how politicians should behave in looking after our interests and our environment.

On Europe, Natalie re-affirmed the party's enthusiasm for working within the EU to transform it into an organisation based on Green principles.

Green parties are a major force in the politics of some of our continental neighbour countries, enjoying a far higher profile than ours has here, where it maintains a modest presence but thankfully growing fast.

I stand somewhere between Farage and Bennett on Europe – like him, I despise the massive influence the political super state is having on our own affairs to our considerable detriment. But, like her, I firmly support close and friendly ties with our neighbours – just so long as we maintain strong elements of our own identity.

And I avidly back the Greens' call for the devolution of power – handing it back to the people at grass-roots level through their locally –elected representatives.

I'm not sure quite where I stand on Scotland's impending historic referendum on national independence. I don't really know enough about the issue to have an informed view. But it does seem that, as usual, there are pros and cons.

While politicians and citizens argue, I just hope and pray that, whatever the outcome; the English and Scottish remain firm friends linked by blood, culture and trade. I feel exactly the same about the Welsh and the Irish.

And I feel strongly that, regardless of national independence, devolution is a far better, more democratic option than further centralisation of power, which puts crucial decision-making in the hands of fewer and fewer people progressively more divorced from the localities they are supposed to be representing.

**March 8** – It's just before midnight and I've spent a great night at The Bell (Seabourne's Bar). I went to see the rock covers band Beyond Redemption, who I'd heard were good.

They were, doing fine versions of Cream, UFO, Animals, Hendrix, Zeppelin, Thin Lizzy and Bad Company songs. That alone would have made it worth turning up.

But, added to that, I saw and chatted to loads of the pub's "old crowd" who had decided to check out the bar, its new management team and the live music all on the same night.
They included Tim Robbins, Bev Jones, Paul Moran, Chris and Lou Davis, Julia Pike, Jim Hannen Davies and Stuart and his

wife Melody.  John Gaynor, Ollie Okoye, Lee Robertson, Billy Clarkson, Chelsea Bob, Jim, my hairdresser Jan, Tamsin and Sam and Dave Lowney were also there.

Good music and good company – sweet!

**March 14** – Legendary left-wing Labour MP Tony Benn has died aged 88.  Love him or hate him, he was without doubt one of the greatest icons of British politics in the second half of the 20th century.

Born Anthony Wedgewood Benn into quite a privileged background, he renounced his peerage to become an ardent socialist and champion of the downtrodden – a thorn in the side of both Conservative opponents and fierce critics in his own party.

Mr Benn – as he insisted on being called - became an MP in November 1950 and served in the cabinets of both Harold Wilson and James Callaghan.

A major figure on the left of the party, he narrowly missed out on the deputy leadership in 1981 and was a popular public speaker, anti-war protester and political diarist.

He supported the 1984 miners' strike and other high-profile campaigns that took on both Tory and Labour governments.

Some Labour supporters claimed he was a very divisive figure in the party and his left-wing stance badly damaged its reputation as an organisation fit for government, helping keep it out of power and on the opposition benches for years.

The fact that Tony Blair won an election after taking the party into the political centre to fight the Tories on their own ground seemed to prove the point.

Benn, in turn, revelled in his "man of the people" role and

despised Blair's New Labour, seeing it as selling out decent and altruistic socialist principles in a mad bid to gain power at all costs.

He served as an MP for more than 50 years and became notorious as a left-wing firebrand with a burning desire to help right the wrongs he saw in the way our country was run. He hated elitism and injustice.

I liked him a lot – he inspired people and spoke a great deal of sense. Some loathed him for his unflinching and defiant style, but others – especially the young, and notably Glastonbury festival-goers – were electrified by his passion, oratory and messages of equality and peace.

While some bitter opponents have stayed quiet, tributes have come in from across the spectrum. Even Cameron grudgingly admitted his admiration for the man's skill as a Parliamentarian and diarist, even though politically they were poles apart.

**March 17** - Happy St Patrick's Day. It would also have been my Pisces pal Pat Jones' birthday, but she sadly passed over a couple of years ago. RIP treasured friend.

Pat - Tom and Carole's mum – was a lovely lady, warm, wise, perceptive witty and funny. She was christened Patricia as she was born on the Irish patron saint's day.

People in Ireland, England, America and other countries will be having a few drinks and partying later today. But in the Ukraine, the situation stays grim and volatile.

This morning's TV news informed us that about 93 per cent of voters in Crimea yesterday backed a move to leave the Ukraine and be re-united with Russia - in other words, being ruled from Moscow, not Kiev.

Crimea was transferred from Russia to the Ukraine 60 years

ago, when both were still part of the old Soviet Union.

There were 1.5 million eligible voters in yesterday's referendum. Officials put the turnout at more than 80%.

So, on the face of it, an overwhelming majority has chosen democratically to leave the Ukraine and re-join Russia.

There's apparently been ethnic tension for decades and passions have been running high.

Crimeans loyal to Kiev boycotted the referendum, and the EU and US both condemned it, saying it was illegal and undemocratic with people voting at gunpoint.

Yesterday's hurriedly-arranged poll was the latest twist in a crisis that's bitterly divided Ukrainians - some wanting more integration with Europe and others rejecting this idea in favour of stronger ties with Russia.

Friction and bloodshed have blighted the country with America, the EU and our own government all supporting the pro-Europeans to the point of threatening sanctions if Russia takes military action in the Ukraine.

But from what we hear about yesterday's vote, it sounds like most Crimeans ally themselves with Russia. According to their new government, anyway.

Both sides claim they're upholding the principle of democracy. It's all pretty confusing. I just hope it's resolved with the minimum of hassle and heartache.

Turning from TV news to TV fiction – apparently different things - there's a fascinating story line in Emmerdale at the moment that poses tricky questions of ethics and morality.

A teenaged character called Belle recently had a blazing row with her best pal Gemma over a lad they're both sweet on. Belle was sober, Gemma drunk – and as Belle pushed her, she lost her balance and fell, hitting her head. It started to bleed.

As Gemma got to her feet again, still arguing, Belle, thinking she was okay, stormed angrily off into the night, heading home. After her departure, her dazed mate fell once more, this time tumbling into a ditch where she lost consciousness, later dying.

Guilt-ridden Belle now wants to come clean to the police and face her punishment.  But her mum and other relatives are trying to stop her, saying it was a very regrettable accident and Gemma was alive, apparently alright, when Belle left her so she shouldn't blame herself too much.

An added complication is that recent friction between the two friends is a well-known fact locally and neighbours and the cops might think Belle meant to harm Gemma, justifying severe punishment.
A major factor in all this is the effect it will have on Belle's family, especially her dad - a big, burly one-time tough guy now ageing fast with serious health issues, emotionally fragile after a mental breakdown.

So far, he's unaware of Belle's extreme torment, perceiving her stressed and moody behaviour as the outward sign of acute grief over her mate's shocking demise.

Strict morality and clear-cut ethics demand that Belle does the generally accepted right thing and tells the truth, salving her own conscience while trusting that police and peers accept her part in the tragedy but don't hold her totally responsible.

But Belle is so grief-stricken and guilt-racked she's not thinking straight. She's convinced she's killed her mate and should pay. In this frame of mind, she could easily implicate herself, ending up with a stricter punishment than she really deserves – especially given the recent history of bad blood between the two girls.

And, in this particular case, we're left asking if confessing would do more harm than good. Nothing can bring her mate back and poor Belle can't change what happened.

Obviously, she should have stayed with her pal and ensured she was okay and made it home. But we can all be wise after the event and it's too late now to rectify her dreadful decision. It's just heartbreaking that the outcome was so serious.

We can all sympathise with Belle – in her shoes, we'd feel the same. But what of her dad – would this tip him over the edge, kill him even? Is it worth risking that while throwing Belle's young life away over what was, in the final analysis, a terrible mishap followed by a disastrous judgement call?

This clever story line shows just how complex some problems are and how making ethical, moral decisions isn't always as cut and dried as we'd like it to be.

**March 18, teatime** – Well, I've had a good day. A group of us went to Days again, the massive Chinese/English restaurant in central Bournemouth.

I went there and back on the bus with Tina Mcauley. While at Days, we hooked up with Sam Excell, Carl Young, their little boys Rudy and Bailey, Sam's daughter Rebecca (Bec), Bec's dad Russell Hall, and our mutual mate Jem Hannen. Nice!

**March 19** – Today is Budget Day, a chance for Chancellor George Osborne to further turn the screw on hard-pressed citizens already suffering from his vicious policies.

It's claimed that unemployment is falling and the economy's slowly recovering. Please excuse me if I laugh out loud at these ridiculous and insulting assertions.

This morning's TV news also told us that a new 12-sided pound coin is to be introduced in 2017. It will look similar to the old threepenny bit we had before decimalisation.

The Crimean crisis rumbles on with tough-talking Russia warning America and Europe that imposing economic sanctions would have unspecified but serious consequences.

And concern is growing over a missing Malaysia Airlines plane with 239 on board. The Boeing 777 disappeared 11 days ago around the Strait of Malacca connecting the Pacific and Indian Oceans.

All sorts of theories abound but there's scant hard evidence to help solve the mystery.

**March 30** – Happy Mother's Day to all my female family members and friends with young or grown-up children.

On a much more sombre note, I have to sadly report the demise of a lovely four-legged pal. Sam's former partner Russell has had to have his Staffie bitch Lola put down because she was suffering from a fast-spreading cancer.

Sam, Russell and their families are devastated and I'm pretty choked myself. Lola was a furry friend of mine. She was so sweet-natured and adorable.

Anyone tempted to chime in here with a daft and insensitive comment like "get a grip, it's only a flipping dog and can easily be replaced" can go jump off a cliff as far as I'm concerned, for they're cold-hearted clots who have clearly never had a canine companion.

In the wider world, AFC Bournemouth – the Cherries – are doing really well at the moment. Promoted to the Championship at the end of last season, they're mid-table and look like they're going to stay up.

It's especially pleasing that they're doing better than rated teams like Birmingham and Leeds, beating both in recent weeks.

Meanwhile, the fate of the missing Boeing plane remains uncertain. After all this time, it seems like its passengers have perished.  It's strange, tragic and worrying.

**April 2** – The Emmerdale story-line about Belle's fatal bust-up has moved on.  She's been charged with murder in scenes which don't show Yorkshire Police in a very good light.

Her father now knows of her predicament and, in a state of shock, actually accompanied her to the cop shop when she secretly handed herself in and confessed – behind the backs and against the advice of other loved ones.

The officers' hard-line, totally over the top, unsympathetic reaction has left him further reeling.

Gemma's dad has heard the news and is furious at Belle and her family. Her confession has stirred up a hornet's nest – just as her protective relatives had predicted.

Her mum is incensed that her dad didn't stop her going to the police.  They're on the point of breaking up, adding to Belle's anguish.

It will be interesting to see how all this pans out.  Surely, common sense will prevail and Belle will be dealt with leniently and sensitively. We all hope so.

And we're comforted by the fact that this is soap land, where things usually sort themselves out in the end.

This intriguing tale has inspired me to write another lyric.  Here it is:

### *Notion of Sin*

*Martin Money, April 2, 2014.*

*Your selfish quest for salvation is wreaking such wide
devastation
The guilt by which you are driven wants closure that you've
been forgiven*

*Your notion of sin is blighting the lives of loved ones and
friends that surround you
Your burning desire is making you blind to impacts on those all
around you*

*Your admirable wish to put it all right is noble but oh so
misguided
The wounds that have healed will open again; the whole will
once more be divided*

*Your selfish quest for salvation is wreaking such wide
devastation
The guilt by which you are driven wants closure that you've
been forgiven.*

*You might feel relieved it's all off your chest, but what of the
turmoil of others?
While you're satisfied, they'll all feel betrayed, hit bad by the
recall that smothers*

*What use will it be to broadcast your act if it means that your
circle is broken?
Your medicine downed, you ease your own mind but it's all just
a damaging token*

*Your selfish quest for salvation is wreaking such wide
devastation
The guilt by which you are driven wants closure that you've
been forgiven.*

Just goes to show how difficult it can be sometimes choosing the best thing to do.  Some would say this is precisely why we need a holy book or list of rules to spell it out in non-ambiguous terms.

I disagree – the longer I live in this plane of existence, the more I realise that life isn't quite like that.  It would be so much easier if everything was always so black and white and clear cut.  But it's not – it's multicoloured and frequently messy.

The Emmerdale story line is so shrewd because it forces the characters – and us - to confront head-on a tough ethical, moral dilemma.

Belle's screwed up, big-time – there's no question of that.  But murder?  I think not.

To me, murder means a cold-blooded, clinical, pre-planned act of extermination – not a tragic death caused by a minor act of violence in the heat of the moment.  Context and mitigating circumstances are crucial in addressing such matters.

And, as I've already said, in this particular instance, Belle should have kept quiet and lived with the painful memory that her actions led in part to Gemma's death.

She deserves to carry that burden for life – but without letting it eat away at her.  In time, she would have learned to move on, eventually forgiving herself while never forgetting her act of extreme recklessness that tragically contributed to a fatality.

Yes, she should have made sure her mate got home.  But would Gemma have died from her head injury anyway?  And was she so intoxicated she would have lost her footing whether or not Belle pushed her?  No-one will ever know.  And that's the crux of the matter.

Belle didn't mean to permanently silence her friend.  She pushed her in a fit of anger. No gun, knife or bat - not even a punch or slap. The fact that Gemma fell was as much her own fault for being so drunk. And she was being obnoxious and just as aggressive as Belle. How the heck can that be classed as murder?

Belle should learn from this bitter life lesson. But she shouldn't be locked up and treated like a ruthless killer.

It should go without saying that my comments about things being messy and far from clear-cut apply mainly to the world as experienced by teenagers and adults.

Children under 12 need to be brought up from infancy with very stringent rules and boundaries – exercised with love, not cruelty of course. Parents who neglect this duty and let their offspring misbehave are doing them no favours and in fact are committing a form of child abuse.

Once the basics are mastered, and as the kids get older and the complexities of life start to hit home, the adults around them should explain with patience and compassion how to negotiate the puzzling moral and ethical minefields they'll face.

That's how it should be, anyway. But when grown ups continue to take the black and white, no colours in between approach themselves like children, the problems come thick and fast.

It doesn't help when they start quoting holy books in a cold, rigid, unrealistic way totally ignoring the complexities and subtleties of human existence.

The huge irony here is that the holy texts themselves can appear riddled with mixed messages and strange inconsistencies.

Take just one example from the Bible. Much is made of the Ten Commandments, one of which states "thou shalt not kill". No riders, no ambiguity. It's crystal clear.

So how on Earth does that square with the Old Testament account of Abraham agreeing to murder his own son as a sacrifice to his God?

Of course, in the end the deity stops him and the boy's life is saved.  The story is intended to show the depth of Abraham's devotion to his Lord.  He's being severely tested – and seemingly passes with flying colours.

But, apart from featuring the ultimate display of bad parenting, this bizarre and disturbing tale appears to defy the holy commandment with God himself suggesting the blood sacrifice. No wonder people get confused and frequently screw up.

**April 4** – Yet another lyric formed itself in my mind last night while I was watching telly.  I wrote it down, and then tidied it up this morning.  It goes thus:


***Grease the Wheels***

*Martin Money, April 3-4, 2014.*


*Grease the wheels, grease the wheels*
*People like you grease the wheels*
*Grease the wheels, grease the wheels*
*People like you grease the wheels*

*I envy your patience and wisdom*
*Compassion shines out from your pores*
*The love and respect that you foster*
*Repairs all division and sores*

*The world so needs such sweet souls as you*
*To heal and unite and bring joy*

*To generate kindness, make others smile*
*And chase off the urge to destroy*

*We really should be less dogmatic*
*The wheels are stuck fast, with cogs static*
*Grease the wheels, grease the wheels,*
*People like you grease the wheels*
*Grease the wheels, grease the wheels*
*People like you grease the wheels*

*The world so needs such sweet souls as you*
*To heal and unite and bring joy*
*To generate kindness, make others smile*
*And chase off the urge to destroy*

*Grease the wheels, grease the wheels,*
*People like you grease the wheels*
*Grease the wheels, grease the wheels*
*People like you grease the wheels.*

Patience and wisdom – yeah, we so badly need both when dealing with our own and each others' flaws and foul-ups. But wisdom from where?

Sacred texts, perceptive sayings and experience of life's unpredictable twists and turns are pretty good starting points.

But when dealing with ancient scriptures, we have to be constantly aware that these were written by equally flawed humans struggling to express profound eternal truths.

They may have been inspired by the divine, imbued with it even, but they were still just people like you and me.

And any original pure intentions will have been filtered through centuries of edits, deletions, amendments, misinterpretations, poor translations, rigid dogma, religious propaganda, political spin and dodgy agendas.

Always be guided by your heart, your gut instinct, your higher self – whatever you want to call it. If you're properly tuned in with it, you should be okay.

I'm saying all this to me as much as anyone else – probably more. Isn't it strange how we can all freely give out good advice but far too rarely follow it ourselves?

**April 6** – Composing a lyric is an intriguing exercise for me. I usually start with a line or phrase, find another to rhyme with it, and off I go. Often these become the first two lines of the song, but sometimes they form the chorus or a part of it.

Frequently I find that, once finished, the best or most important line of the whole piece is one I've only initially thought of to rhyme with something else.

This can even become the work's title as my imagination takes off and the creation takes on a life of its own, ending up heading in a direction I didn't envisage when I began the process.

Take that last lyric, "Grease the Wheels". The seed and starting point was the phrase "I envy your patience and wisdom." I carried on with a rough version up to the word "dogmatic." Needing something to rhyme, I came up with "cogs static."

That set me following a train of thought about the wheels of society being jammed, needing lubrication, and I formulated what ultimately became the chorus and title.
I hadn't anticipated this at all, but it seemed to work and the piece - although still a bit ragged and disjointed - held together okay.

So I changed a few words to tidy and tighten it up, and the entire lyric, started from scratch during an evening, was completed by lunchtime the following day.

**April 8** – Veteran actor Mickey Rooney has died at the age of 93.  He appeared in more than 200 films in a career spanning almost nine decades.

Starting off very young in the era of silent movies, he quickly became world-famous appearing alongside screen legends including the young starlets Judy Garland and Liz Taylor.

He also did television, radio, Broadway and vaudeville. One of his last performances was a cameo with the Muppets in 2011.

**April 9** – Oh dear – another death in the entertainment world. This time it's Peaches Geldof, daughter of Sir Bob and the late Paula Yates, who has passed on aged just 25.  Her body was found at her Kent home on Monday and a post mortem is being held later today (Wednesday).

It could take some weeks for the results to be known and the need for an inquest to be gauged. Police say that her death was "non-suspicious but unexplained and sudden".

Peaches Geldof had two young sons with her second husband, musician Tom Cohen. She was 11 when her own TV presenter mother died.

Her rock star father, knighted in 1986 for his work in organising Live Aid and other concerts that raised millions for the starving people of Africa, said the family was "beyond pain."

He added that Peaches was "the wildest, funniest, cleverest, wittiest and the most bonkers of all of us."

Irish President Michael D Higgins, actress Susan Sarandon and singer Boy George have been among those adding their tributes to the popular writer, TV presenter and model.

I didn't really know that much about her, but she was clearly loved and respected by many. So, it seems, we've lost another good 'un.

Speaking of which, it's sometimes said that prophets are not always recognised in their own lands. That's a pity, for if more were, we'd live in a far nicer place.

Occasionally someone comes along who exudes love and wisdom, inspiring people to unite, smile and care. Guys like Y'shua (Jesus), Krishna, Buddha, Muhammad (Mohammed) and Meher Baba spring immediately to mind.

Saint Francis, the Dalai Lama, Ghandi and a host of gurus also serve this positive purpose.

Then there are those who, though just as flawed as the rest of us, carry good vibes in the messages they bring – such as Carl Jung, John Lennon, Bob Marley, Albert Einstein, William Blake, Bill Hicks, Pete Townsend, Graham Nash, George Harrison and Donovan.

The massive problem is that people like this don't run the show. That's left to sleazy politicians with suspect agendas firmly rooted in a material world riddled with vested interests, corruption and greed.

Our leaders don't lead by example – they get up to all sorts of dodgy antics while coming down hard on ordinary citizens who dare to do the same.

Apart from the Peaches Geldof tragedy, the other big news item in today's media has been Maria Miller's resignation as culture secretary in a furore over her expenses claims.

There's huge speculation that the government closed ranks and forced her out – despite her assertion that it was her decision to go faced with all the adverse publicity that she said was distracting people from the coalition's "incredible achievements."

Apart from asking what incredible achievements, I deeply suspect pressure was put on her to quit as she was proving a headache and a vote loser with local and European elections looming next month and a general election on the horizon too.

Mrs Miller was cleared of funding a home for her parents at taxpayers' expense, but was told to repay £5,800 of the expenses she claimed.

The independent parliamentary commissioner for standards had previously recommended she repay £45,000.

But the lower sum was approved by the Commons Standards Committee, which has the final say on whether to accept the commissioner's recommendations - a decision which sparked a backlash across the political spectrum and calls for changes in how complaints against MPs are investigated.

Mrs Miller apologised in the Commons, but was criticised for the brevity of the statement she made. In a TV interview, she pointed out that she was cleared of the central allegation made about her by a Labour MP.

The scandal surrounding her expenses claims is without doubt a major embarrassment for Prime Minister David Cameron, who has gone on record demanding long prison sentences for benefit cheats.

Double standards are rife, it seems. I'm sure I'm not alone in thinking that deliberately defrauding the system is wrong –

whether the culprits are welfare claimants, tax dodgers or MPs.

Wrongdoers should all be treated the same in my opinion – and Parliamentarians caught breaking the rules need to be dealt with as harshly or leniently as anyone else.

Green MP Caroline Lucas was recently arrested and taken to court for participating in a peaceful protest over fracking. Yet MPs – and bankers, for that matter - face no such heavy law enforcement when they cheat the system to reap financial benefits, it seems. And I find that unpalatable.

**April 17** – It's Thursday and it's been a lovely sunny week so far – in fact, so nice and warm that my friends Sam and Carl had their first barbeque of the season on Tuesday in their freshly spruced-up garden.

Its Easter weekend so they're planning another one to welcome back Sam's son Alex, who yesterday returned to Bournemouth with his new girlfriend Charley after a few months working as a chef in Oxfordshire.

It's my Auntie Joyce's birthday today.  Not sure how old she is, but she must be in her nineties by now.

I've just phoned her to wish her well and a few days ago I popped some money in a card and posted it to her. She received them okay and thanked me for both.

She does the same for me on my birthday but we haven't seen each other face to face for years as she's infirm, doesn't go out and is a bit funny about having visitors.

On the international front, mayhem and misery continue to plague Syria and the Ukraine and the search goes on for that missing passenger plane.

Nine people have been confirmed dead and 287 people are still missing after a South Korean ferry capsized.

Coastguards say 174 people have been rescued so far. But high winds and rough seas have proven troublesome.

The ferry, with 462 people and 150 vehicles on board, was sailing to the southern island of Jeju yesterday when it sent a distress call at 9am local time (1am UK time) as it began listing to one side.

Within two hours it had completely capsized, with only the front part of its hull visible above the water. The distraught captain today apologized unreservedly as the salvage mission continued. Many of the passengers were students.

Closer to home, the government is up to its tricks again, making chillingly cold-hearted and stunningly ridiculous statements.

The latest gold nugget of callous stupidity is its call for pensioners to be given a life expectancy forecast to help them manage their finances in retirement.

Since when have accountants, tax advisors, or even doctors had the gift of premonition?

Granted, a non-smoker who keeps their drinking to sensible levels, avoids fatty foods, exercises and leads a so-called healthy lifestyle is theoretically giving themself a better chance to live longer.

But they could be hit by a bus tomorrow, while someone who's been given the alarming news that they don't have long left might actually survive way beyond a forecast death date.

Some people pass away in their fifties and sixties, others in their seventies, eighties and nineties, and there are no guarantees one way or the other.

Sadly, we all need money to survive. Many rely on a regular income, the lucky or prudent have savings, certain people will have both, others neither.

And those reaching retirement age will be in a variety of circumstances - dictated as much by chance as any attempts at forward planning. Many variables come into play – state of health, company pensions, cash in the bank, fickle fortune and so on.

A reasonable state pension should be made available to those who need it. And fiscal safety nets have to be in place to ensure those without the means to support themselves still get the basics of a decent standard of living.

But instead of showing respect towards senior citizens and a desire to recognise and honour their decades of service to society, our current crop of political masters seems keen to dodge responsibility in a brash display of patronising buck-passing.

Looks to me like this latest stunt is just another stick to beat us with – another way to scare and control us. A blunt expiry date forecast could be terrifying for some, causing them acute concern and possibly even hastening their demise.

Not that this lot in government cares – for them it will mean a few less people to look after and a slightly smaller state pension bill.
It's sinister in the extreme – positively Orwellian - and typical

of this brutal coalition's hard line approach to running our beloved country in its own twisted way.

**April 18** – It's Good Friday – but far from good for the victims of the ferry disaster and their families. The death toll has reached 28 so far as the rescue attempts continue.

It's also a bad day in Nepal, where at least 12 people have died in an avalanche on the slopes of Mount Everest.

Some climbers have been rescued while others are still missing in the worst tragedy on the mountain.

Also in the news, Green MP Caroline Lucas has been acquitted of wilful obstruction and a public order offence while taking part in a protest against fracking at Balcombe, West Sussex, last summer.

Good – for in my mind what she did during a lawful and peaceful demonstration was nothing compared to the disgraceful behaviour of other MPs in bending the rules, fiddling their expenses and getting up to all sorts of devious and dishonest activities.

I can't help thinking that Caroline was targeted - mainly because in 2010 she famously became the country's first Green MP and rival politicians need her to be discredited.

Fracking is the highly controversial method of extracting gas by pumping water and potentially toxic chemicals underground at high pressure.

Supporters, including the government (surprise, surprise!), claim it's a cheap and efficient way of accessing energy that cuts people's fuel bills.

But opponents, including environmental campaign group Friends of the Earth, say it causes pollution, destabilises the land – increasing the threat of small earthquakes – aggravates climate change and intensifies the risk of drinking water contamination.

I know who I tend to believe!


***************************************

# CHAPTER TWO – MYTHS AND LEGENDS

**April 21** – Wishing a very happy third birthday to my grandson, Lucas. It's also Easter Monday and I've had a blinding weekend.

Friday I went to a great barbie at Sam and Carl's, with them, Alex and Bec, Rudy, Bailey, Kelly Adams, her daughter Storm, Sharon Pendleton, Russell Hall, Jem Hannen, Jimmy, his daughter Molly, Ryan Millen and Alex's girlfriend Charley.

Saturday I had a quiet evening at home to recuperate but last night I went to The Bell and thoroughly enjoyed a fab session with several mates – John Gaynor, Jem Hannen, his daughter Martine, Jem's nephew Stuart and his wife Melody, Kelly Adams, her friend Gemma, Billy Clarkson, Matthew Brant and his partner Dani, Clare Hayes and Mark Hemington.

Turning briefly to the news, Prime Minister David Cameron has apparently put his foot in it yet again – over religion this time.

He is quoted as saying that Britain should be "more confident about our status as a Christian country."

The timing is interesting, coming as it does during one of the two biggest annual festivals honouring Jesus.

More than 50 writers, scientists, broadcasters and academics, including author Terry Pratchett, performer Tim Minchin, journalist Polly Toynbee, philosopher A. C. Grayling and presenter Dan Snow, have signed a protest letter to the Daily Telegraph.

They say his comment was divisive and he risked causing alienation in our multi-faith society.

Well, apart from pointing out that Britain is actually an alliance of countries, I wonder why on Earth he said anything at all.

Let's face it - he was in a no-win situation. Some would have objected just as strongly if he'd recognised the reality of our 21st century diverse religious nature. He should have kept his mouth shut.

Granted, England, Scotland, Wales and Ireland are historically, traditionally and arguably still primarily Christian nations. (Just like many others across the globe).

But followers of other faiths, pagans and atheists living in the British Isles would be rightly offended by Cameron's clumsy statement.

For my part, I wish you all a very happy Easter. Like Christmas, it's become an occasion for people to eat, drink and celebrate, regardless of their chosen religion. And what's so wrong with that? Any excuse for a party and a bit of communal bonding I say!

But seriously, though – if people want to use these events to re-affirm their beliefs, fine, especially if those beliefs then spur them on to do good works benefiting their peers and their communities.

In other words, just so long as their faith – be it Christian, Jewish, Muslim, pagan, Hindu, Buddhist or whatever – ends up as an instrument of compassion, tolerance and harmony, not friction, division, and alienation.

Tragically, religious nuts from all sides far too often generate the latter negative vibes.

And Jesus followers of various persuasions choose to ignore the fact that, rather like Christmas, most of the main features of this festival are actually pagan in origin and have little or nothing to do with Christianity.

Church leaders decided centuries ago to mark their Lord's birth and resurrection at times coinciding with pre-existing festivals honouring the winter solstice and spring equinox.

I guess this was to make the transition to their faith easier, seeing as people were already used to celebrating then.

The chocolate eggs and cute bunnies are in fact modern versions of ancient fertility symbols. Death and resurrection tales recur in belief systems pre-dating Christianity.

Even the word Easter is strikingly similar to the names of two pagan goddesses, the Anglo-Saxon Eostre and Babylonian Ishtar.

And the occasion's fluctuating dates, varying from year to year, reflect the changing phases of the moon – an ancient and oft-used religious icon that plays a huge role in paganism, Judaism and Islam, a lot more than it does in modern Christianity.

Or is this just a load of old tosh – ill-informed mischief-making intended to discredit a revered and sacred tradition? Depends where you stand on matters religious, I guess.

All I'm saying is that various interpretations can be put on ancient texts and customs - but way too many people are blinkered, inflexible, stubborn and intolerant.

Me? - I'll continue to stick by my assertion that all faiths hold sparkling jewels of pure wisdom but none has a monopoly on truth. And – shock, horror, even atheists can come up with wonderfully unifying concepts and flashes of profound insight.

I just think it's ludicrous, frustrating, tragic and bitterly ironic that religions have become such highly divisive and ultimately lethal systems of ruthless control instead of being the positive forces of healing and harmony their founders intended.

No-one has any right to knock another's beliefs – with one crucial proviso.  And this is that they're not using those beliefs to harm, belittle or bully others.  Respect your neighbour's choices and agree to differ rather than lurch into battle and bloodshed.

For in the end, we are all one – all species and organisms, at one with the universe, all part of the eternal One.  That's the bottom line as far as I'm concerned.  But egos and false concepts of individuality cause us to feel isolated.

This is extremely scary, so, in a desperate bid to be part of something, we align ourselves to factions of like-minded people who share our views but strongly oppose those of others similarly bonding together under a different banner.

Results? -  Friction, stark separation, hurt and tragedy.  The human condition.  We need to find ways to reverse this situation and rediscover our deeply buried instinct for unity and peace.

**April 23** – Happy St George's Day...hell yeah! Should it become a national holiday? I dunno, but it's certainly an appropriate occasion to honour our beloved motherland – minus any ugly traces of racism or bigotry, that is.

Being English doesn't necessarily mean you're blue-eyed or fair-skinned.  And you certainly don't need to be a raving elitist with a superior and jingoistic attitude, as some would have us believe.  It applies to anyone born in this country – yes, anyone, regardless of colour, faith or cultural background.

Let's get it straight. People have been coming from overseas and merging with existing communities here for centuries. We're a mixed blood nation and have been for countless generations.

It's high time we recognised this truth and claimed back our national flag and patron saint from unhinged right-wing crazies who'd drag them through the mud and blood.

It's also vital that we appreciate that those born in other countries can also love their homelands just as passionately - just so long as no-one corrupts this passion into a destructive frenzy.

Sod corrosive nationalism, we're all Homo sapiens, dammit!

By the way, it's also Shakespeare's birthday. Whether or not the Bard of Avon actually wrote the brilliant literature carrying his name, he's known all over the world as an English icon.

Just like St George himself, whose real identity – and even nationality - is also a subject for heated debate.

It's widely accepted that his father was Greek or Turkish and he was probably born in Palestine, thought to be his mother's homeland, in the third century. The date of his birth is disputed but it's said he died a Christian martyr on April 23 by our calendar.

His flag – a red cross on a white background – also represents England. And it's used in various other countries and cities where he's similarly their patron saint.

In Palestine, he's regarded as a national hero who opposed the persecution of fellow Christians. He is said to have served in the Roman army.

While the Western world marks St George's Day on 23 April, in the Palestinian areas it falls on 6 May, according to an older calendar used by the Eastern Churches.

The saint is said to have given away all his possessions and remained true to his Christian faith when imprisoned, tortured and finally executed.

As to the dragon he's said to have slain, is this a metaphor for a brutal, oppressive regime he's considered to have been fighting against? Who knows? – The whole story is shrouded in myth and mystery.

Religious literature and familiar folk tales are drenched in deep symbolism, often misunderstood. Various interpretations can be put on them.

Was Saint George as he's portrayed real or legend? Is Shakespeare in truth the genius who wrote those marvellous plays and sonnets? The arguments will rage on.

Vital historical facts are being altered daily thanks to the Internet. Important ancient texts have been destroyed by accident and warfare. Facts have been obscured over the centuries by fiction.

In many cases this is a deadly serious business. But when it comes to the bard and the saint, maybe not so important. Regardless of truth and accuracy, one has become an emblem of literary and dramatic excellence, the other of courage and compassion.

The works attributed to Shakespeare stand on their own. So do the stories told about Saint George.

We need such shining examples to inspire others to emulate the best in human endeavour. In these particular cases, does it really matter if the details are correct?

And in the final analysis, where we are born is also neither here nor there.

It's far more important that, wherever it is, and whatever the circumstances, we are brought up in a loving, nurturing, stable, non-judgemental and calm environment rooted in the sterling values of compassion, tolerance and mutual respect.

That way, we hopefully grow into decent, well-adjusted adults, not damaged, bitter, angry casualties with scores to settle and axes to grind.

**April 24** – Hot on the heels of Cameron's pointed and inflammatory statement about Britain being a "Christian country", we now have former Labour PM Tony Blair weighing in with an equally insensitive and insulting warning over what he calls "radical Islam."

Speaking in London yesterday, he said that such extremism still represented the biggest threat to global security in the 21st century. It was holding back development across Africa and the Far East.

Seems to me he wants us to believe there's a dangerous network of terrorist groups hell bent on causing disruption wherever possible, determined to replace democracy and freedom of choice with the iron-fist enforcement of a single, world-wide, brutal and retrograde religious system miles away from the original message of Islam.

I despise extremism of any kind, political or religious. The venomous rants and murderous acts of fanatical Muslims horrify me just as much as those of unhinged Christian nuts - or zealots of any kind, for that matter. But look who's saying this.

A man who betrayed his party's socialist roots to seize power, became progressively more right-wing and high-handed in government, and unforgivably used 911 as an excuse to invade

Iraq and Afghanistan - and all while claiming to be a Christian!

Bold statements like those he made yesterday do nothing to help and in fact fan the flames of division and conflict – angering and radicalising formerly moderate Muslims. Just like his "God's on our side" claims over the wars he declared.

In turn, hard line Islamic hate-mongers turn one-time moderate Christians against all Muslims as the madness spreads and blood-letting increases.

All this is abhorrent to the vast majority of followers of both faiths who are decent, tolerant peace-loving people who don't want to fight anyone.

And then you get the anti-terrorism police, who today appealed to British Muslim women to try and stop their men joining the fight in Syria's blood-stained civil war.

Sure, it's very alarming when those who start out with a desire to build a better world end up brainwashed and radicalised by twisted versions of their religious beliefs. People suffer and die in ideological clashes that last for centuries – millennia even.

And it's so, so tragically ironic when you consider that Jesus preached turning the other cheek while Islam accepts him as a prophet and promotes religious tolerance.

If you return to the source scriptures, you'll find far purer and kinder versions of these faiths than those peddled by firebrand zealots through the ages.

Gordon Bennett - there's even been raging debates and bitter rivalries within the religions themselves. How insane is that?

Somewhere along the line, divine wisdom has been lost and altruistic intentions badly obscured as believers have gone off at tangents, driven by their own warped ideas -heavily influenced by control freaks with vested interests and political agendas.

It seems to me that Cameron's comments, Blair's warning and the counter-terrorist coppers' appeal are among the latest features of a concerted and sinister effort to demonize certain groups and up the stakes in an ongoing, lethal ideological war.

It's so incessant that people become hostile towards all Muslims. The same applies to Poles, Romanians and others minority groups constantly mentioned in the media. And they, in turn, become hostile towards us. It freezes my blood – it really does!

Is there an element of truth in Blair's nasty network allegation? Quite possibly. There are networks all over the place – social, business, communication, and, yes, terrorist.

In fact, networks make a lot of sense as a means of bringing people together. This can be for a variety of reasons - personal, financial, religious, political and so on.

They can be used to exchange resources and intelligence in a mutual drive towards a shared vision. And they can be very beneficial if used for positive purposes – such as helping citizens find love and companionship or assisting charities to co-operate in easing people's suffering.

The jet black flip side of this is that they can just as easily be put to work for negative, disruptive and highly destructive reasons – to frighten, exploit, harm and control people, destabilise society or bring about violent revolution.

A warning about evil terrorist networks can therefore be fully justified - depending on who's issuing it and how it's phrased.

I might have accepted Blair's statement if someone else had said it and it had been a more general warning.

But his inclusion of the word "Islam" made it a very deliberate attack on Muslims in particular – inflammatory and provocative. Just as he intended.

And the fact that it was him saying it turned my stomach, given his record.

There are those who firmly believe that Tony B himself is a member of a sinister network of selfish, greedy, nasty people determined to organise the world for their own benefit while brutally exploiting and depriving others.

But I suspect it could be bigger and wider than that, and there's certainly mileage in the idea that all of us, including politicians and terrorists, are just pawns of a dark ruling elite running the whole show from the shadows.

It's said these odious undesirables orchestrate apparently unconnected events on a global scale as they pull everyone's strings, causing division and conflict so no-one notices that they're keeping all the power and most of the wealth to themselves.

Conspiracy theory cobblers? Maybe it is. I have my suspicions but I'll keep an open mind. It certainly would explain a lot of the confusion, inconsistencies, inequalities, mixed messages, conflict and misery involved in living on this messed-up planet.

Some would call me a gullible fool for even giving such ideas the time of day. They'd accuse me of crazy talk. But I refuse to be blinkered any longer and meekly accept all I'm told. My heart burns too much with unanswered questions.

**April 26** – Oh dear! My beloved Manchester United has sacked manager David Moyes after only 10 months of a six-year contract.

Former Everton boss Moyes took over when the stunningly

successful Sir Alex Ferguson retired, ending a glittering 26-year career during which he'd guided the team to win 38 trophies including 13 Premier League titles and the Champions League cup in 1999 and 2008.

It was nigh on impossible to follow this, but Moyes has had a miserable time. The club is ending the season with no silverware at all and too low in the league points table to qualify for the Champions League next season – for the first time since 1990.

Under Moyes, the team lost six league games at home, was beaten in the FA Cup by Swansea at Old Trafford and went out of the Capital One Cup at the semi-final stage.

With four games to go, United legend Ryan Giggs – the most decorated player in English football – has taken over as caretaker boss until a more permanent replacement can be found.

The team is guaranteed to record its lowest points tally since winning the first ever Premier League title in 1993.

Things came to a head for Moyes last Sunday when United suffered a humiliating 2-0 defeat at – Everton.

I think the club has been a bit hasty – it always takes time for a new manager to settle in. And let's not forget that the great Sir Alex himself was on the point of getting the push when he turned it around spectacularly after a dismal and frustrating start in management at United.

The directors were confident enough of Moyes' abilities to offer him a six-year contract. To turn on him so quickly is hardly fair in my view. But it's a big club with high expectations of success.

Ending a season with no trophies is unpalatable. Missing out on the Champions' League is seen as especially galling – a financial and footballing disaster.

I wish Moyes well in his future career and hope United can weather the storm and get back on track soon, recovering stability, winning matches and lifting silverware again.

**April 27** – My Uncle Fred was a funny bloke. In a good way – laugh-inducing, not weird. Although not blood related, he certainly shared the Money sense of humour.

When I was a kid, he would visit our family home with his wife – Auntie Joyce, Dad's sister – and, after exchanging pleasantries and maybe a joke or two, he'd hunt out my latest batch of comics and settle in a chair to read them all cover to cover. You wouldn't hear a peep out of him for about and hour.

When talking, he'd deliberately get his words wrong, calling Wednesday "Wensbury" and, if it was raining he'd say it was "persisting down."

After yawning, he'd declare, "I've been up all day, you know!" regardless of the time.

Dad and my Uncles Bert and Jack – Joyce's other brothers – were also very funny men so when they and Fred were present we were guaranteed a good time with lots of wise cracks and smiles.

We used to take days out together and meet in each others' homes. During one gathering at Joyce and Fred's, there was a slide show of family photos.

But Fred put one of the slides in the projector sideways by mistake. The picture was of a group of us stood shoulder to shoulder - a typical family shot. But as the image appeared on the screen, we were horizontal, as if balancing on top of each other.

Quick as a flash, Uncle Jack asked: "How did you pile 'em up like that, Fred?", causing us all to dissolve in fits of laughter.

Sadly, all four men have now passed on. They were warm, kind souls who'd much rather see the humorous side of things than stay straight-faced and moan. I try to do the same.

And, despite all the heartache and hassles, I've had plenty to smile about. Many golden memories of family get-togethers and excursions, plus loads of brilliant times with a variety of friends for starters.

Some of them were spent with school mates including Steve Mitchell, John Clow, Steve Burton, Dave Thomas, Terry Stannett, Christopher Zabel and Chris Timber.

Then there were the Domino years when I played in our amateur group touring local churches, clubs and halls in the Slough area playing a wide variety of music and having a ball.

The group's constant members were Rob Bertie, his sister Icilma and me. Lynne Hopton, Gloria O'Connor, June Higginbottom and Beryl Keep were also in the line-up at different times. Lynne's brother John became a very good friend of mine.

In young adulthood, I fondly recall trips to discos at the Top Rank Suite, Reading, with my mate Steve Cooper – even though our attempts to pick up girls were pathetic.

I also had some good laughs with Kevin Fiske, a fellow cub reporter on the Maidenhead Advertiser. And on moving to Dorset, I spent some great times with Torben Lee and Robin Thompkins, two colleagues on local weekly newspapers here.

I've mentioned Torben before – we became really close buddies after discovering we shared a passion for the Beatles. But I haven't yet referred to his political views.

A one-time Marxist, he had mellowed somewhat by the time we met.  A proud card-carrying member of the Labour Party, he was still very much to the left of the movement. He idolised Tony Benn.

Robin was the exact opposite.  Tongue-in-cheek, he'd describe himself as "two goose-steps to the right of Genghis Khan."

He and Torben were always arguing about politics but in truth they were loyal and devoted friends.  Outsiders couldn't understand how two guys apparently so violently at odds could even bear to be in the same room together.  I thought this hilarious.

Work hassles aside, the three of us had a lot of fun.

Robin loved his wordplay. Our editor at the time was a guy called Alex Cummings – vertically challenged, like me. One of Robin's best was "every firm has its shortcomings (short Cummings) – he's ours!"

It was through Torben that I met my treasured friend Shaz – my "faith healer."

Then there were the old Pinecliff pub and Home Guard Social Club days with my second generation Teddy boy pals Tom Jones, Steve Gray, Andy Bethune and Jerry Dean.  Tom's lady Christine, later his wife, their sisters Carole and Linda and Andy's brother Neil were among other members of the fluctuating gang.

So was a guy called Peter Painter, another old-style rock'n'roll fan who hitched up with a lass called Cheryl Collins, who in turn introduced me to her twin sister Josette. They later became our wives but sadly neither relationship lasted.

That was also my first introduction to my good mate Sam Excell – at that time still a girl. I didn't really know her back then, apart from the facts that she had long black hair (still does) and used to baby-sit for Tom and Chris.

But I did know her dad Jim, another Home Guard regular, in passing and everyone knew her Uncle "Cess", who was the bar manager.

Our group also had some fab times in other local pubs such as the Portman (still there), the White Horse (gone) and the Palmerston (gone).

Tom, a workman and deejay, put on disco shows, initially rock'n'roll, in all of them as well as the Home Guard (gone), Pinecliff (gone) Viscount Club (gone) Boscombe Conservative Club (still there) and its Royal British Legion Club (still there).

Other haunts were Boscombe's Salisbury Bars, now Green's, Cromwell's night club, formerly Roxy's (also gone), and Bournemouth's Hop Inn bar for live rock'n'roll.

Tom expanded his repertoire to also do birthday, wedding and special occasion discos all over the area. We were his roadies, helping him lug the equipment in an out of venues. I had to be careful not to put my weak back out. They were great times!

Various others were also involved on these occasions including Tom's mum and dad and his other sister Kate, who all used to come down from Liverpool to visit.

Carole ended up moving here but Linda stayed a short while before returning to her native Manchester. Carole later moved back home to Liverpool, where she still is.

Tom's parents, Pat and Chris, kindly put me up now and then when I drove Tom and Chris to Liverpool for week-long visits. I loved those times – I was made to feel so welcome by the Jones family and their relatives and friends.

I also got a chance to visit Mathew Street, home of the Cavern Club, Beatles Shop and Grapes pub where the fab four used to drink between their sessions at the original Cavern that was just along the road but has now been demolished.

When I got together with Joe, I spent some very pleasant weekends in Salisbury with her parents and wider family before she moved to Bournemouth to be with me and Cheryl, who'd relocated here a couple of years previously.

We also went to Wales a few times to visit Joe's aunt and uncle, Freda and Wayne – a jovial feller who was always laughing.

Later fond memories after my marriage ended include touring Bournemouth late night music and dance venues such as Poet's Corner, the Exchange and Park Lane, formerly the Midnight Express.

These trips were usually made with Kerry Smith – a barmaid at Poet's for a while – and Claire Kimber. Various other people joined us at times including our mutual mates Theresa Bevis, John Gaynor, Paul Moran and a guy who liked to be called Ski.

He hated his real first name Simon so just used the last three letters of his Polish surname.

As to my own name, I'm usually called Martin but a few people –including Kerry, Claire, Gary "Gadget" Preston and Big Sam (Kevin Sansom) – call me Mart.  School friends did too.  Plus my sisters and even my parents – unless I was in trouble!

I don't mind which name people use but most pick the longer version.  That's what's on my birth certificate and I've been called a lot worse!

Anyway, coming more up to date with my nostalgic ramblings, I have had many terrific times at The Bell, my local for ages now, with an ever-changing cast of lovable loons. Claire worked there for many years and Kerry did too on and off.

I've also had some great at-home booze and silliness sessions with Steve Yarwood and Jem Hannen, enjoyed wine and hilarity evenings at Bev Jones' flat, and had several classic nights at Sam Excell's old home in Christchurch Road, Pokesdown.

Jem, Steve, Carl, Linda Franceschi, Roz Tidiman, Mark "Tich" Hemington, Tina and Jeff McNally, Tony Hannen, John Gaynor and Tina Mcauley were among those taking part at Sam's. Other friends attended Bev's "Tuesday night club" meetings.

I've had some really pleasant meals out and cracking drinking sessions with my former workmates at Krypton/Mace such as Lorna Lane, Sue Bolton, June Wade, Lisa, Patsy, Lyn, Noreen and Faron – can't remember their surnames.

I've already told about some of my longer excursions in other books, such as that crazy "Bell on tour" week in Devon, the trip to Hamelin in Germany and the 10-day break to Austria and southern Germany taking in the Oberammergau Passion Play.

Also weekend breaks in Paris and Jersey with the Home Guard crowd and the Butlins holiday camp long weekends in Minehead and Bognor Regis with Claire Kimber and Tina Wilkins. And wine, video and chat sessions with Tina at her old home and visits to London with Kerry, Claire and John Gaynor.

One particular trip to East Ham – Kerry's home area -  was notable for Claire, not the greatest football fan in the world, singing "Stick your blue flag up you're arse" in the Boleyn pub with a load of West Ham fans before their team played Chelsea.

And, of course, that fantastic day out with Kerry and Paul Savage to Manchester United's stadium Old Trafford, the theatre of dreams.

Yep, all in all I've had a right old time in between long bouts of drudgery and hassle in various work places.  I'm happy now to settle in a quieter groove and reminisce.

I've never been a big fan of travelling and these days I only do very short bus trips on my own and slightly longer journeys with company. I lack confidence to be more ambitious and would get too stressed out – not good for my heart.

Over-cautious and a bit silly? Maybe, but I'm happy like this and I'm still having some great times, constantly adding to my store of golden memories.  Sweet!

At one time I knocked around with a guy called Terry who I met through Torben and Sharon.  He was a strange feller, frequently the butt of piss-takes, but Shaz had a soft spot for him and was very protective.

Terry and I ended up spending quite a lot of time together – by default really, as other friends were often off doing whatever they were elsewhere without us.

I was still quite new to this area and by then only had a handful of mates locally.

Most people gave Terry a wide berth, not wanting to get too close. After all, he clearly had mental issues and had at one time been incarcerated in Rampton, one of England's three high-security hospitals. I only know that because Shaz told me.

But I don't know why – I never asked. He was always fine towards me – if a bit desperate and demanding sometimes - and, I thought, if he wanted to tell me, he would. It didn't matter – he treated me okay and that was good enough for me.

The problem came as I tried to increase my social circle. A new pal called Kevin Flynn invited me to a party at his house – so long as I didn't take Terry. Kevin shared the general view that he was an odd feller and thought he'd put people off.

I faced an awkward dilemma – to be loyal to Terry, who I'd known a bit longer, or attend the party and socialise with more people, building up my list of friends. I did the latter, not telling Terry, though I felt horrible doing so.

Did I betray my friend? Looked at one way, clearly I did. But through Kevin I met Tom, and then my social life took off big time.

Tom introduced me to Steve and Andy, then Christine, Carole, Pat and Chris, Linda, and the Home Guard crowd, including Peter. Through him I met Cheryl, then Joe.

Arguably, none of that would have happened had I chosen Terry over Kevin. My life could have turned out completely differently.

I ended up being really good mates with Torben and Shaz – but when they were an item and wanted time on their own; I spent more time with Terry.

In truth, he never was as close a mate.  Often we were on different wavelengths. But he was company when no-one else was around – important for this new kid in town.

But he was very possessive and got jealous when I tried to speak to others. I don't think it any coincidence that after I made that fateful decision over the party, my social life started to blossom.

It grieves me very much that I was such a git towards Terry. I hate being disloyal to mates.  And he had done me no harm. But I look at all the things that happened after that, and I can't help thinking I made the right choice.

Just goes to show how one crucial decision can end up changing your life forever – like in that film, Sliding Doors.  If you've not seen it, do – it's brilliant and very thought-provoking.

I can now see that Terry would have held me back and I might have ended up resenting him for it.  The way things turned out, I got closer to others while he slipped into the background – especially when even Shaz tired of his possessive and jealous streak and started avoiding him.

As times passed and my circumstances evolved I lost contact altogether.  I haven't seen him about for years.  I often wonder where he is and what he's doing now.

Changing the subject completely, I detest it when I see anyone being bullied or terrorised.  But when it involves children or animals it really makes me seethe.

Exploitation, abuse, neglect or cruelty towards youngsters or innocent creatures is deplorable.

It's bad enough when adult humans are the victims – and here our current government is a major offender.  But when it's kids or animals, that's far worse.
Having said that, as always, circumstances, context, motive and seriousness are key factors in deciding what punishment is suitable.

The penalty should be much harsher if blatant brutality and cold control are evident and far more lenient if there's a muddled morality or misguided mindset at work.

Talking of penalties, Wayne Rooney scored from the spot to start Man United's 4-0 rout of Norwich yesterday that gave Ryan Giggs a fine start to his tenure as temporary manager after David Moyes' sacking.

Let's hope this is the beginning of the team's comeback and a return to the road of winning trophies again.

**April 28** – Publicist Max Clifford has been found guilty of eight indecent offences against women and girls.

The 71-year-old, from Surrey, was said to have committed the assaults over a period of almost 20 years. He's been released on bail pending sentencing.

I can't help thinking "serves you right."  This guy's made a career out of washing other people's dirty linen in public as a hard-nosed journalist and media man.

Also in today's news, there's been more about allegations of sexual abuse of boys by the late Cyril Smith, high-profile Liberal Democrat MP who died in 2010 aged 82.

And three generations of the same family, including a nine-week-old baby and two young children, have been killed in a house fire in Sheffield. How tragic.

**April 29** – Happy birthday Bailey, Sam and Carl's youngest boy, who's two today. I'm off to theirs later for a little party in his honour.
And I'll be wearing some of the clothes I recently bought from my local branch of Primark. This is an excellent store where you can get good, fashionable stuff at rock-bottom prices.

I've always begrudged paying too much for clothing and for years I've got quality items from charity shops – a brilliant idea benefiting both low-income people and those the charities support.

But then Primark came along with a wide range of brand new clothes at equally low prices. I've got quite a lot from its Boscombe shop in recent times.

Imagine my horror, then, to learn a few days ago that Primark items are apparently made in Indian sweat shops little better than concentration camps.

It's said that children as young as 11 are put to work for long days by callous bosses in brutal and squalid conditions, sewing tiny beads and sequins on to cheap t-shirts by candle-light for the equivalent of 60p a day.

Some people now boycott Primark stores because of this dreadful revelation. Well lucky them to have enough money that they can be so choosy!

For many, this company has proven a godsend in providing low-income families with new clothes at affordable prices. In an area like Boscombe this is vital – especially with our coalition government turning the financial screws on hard-pressed citizens.

The better-off can easily boycott Primark without losing out themselves.  But many others face a stark choice – buy from there or miss out.

It's a cruel old world when we're encouraged to believe that the only way to produce cheap clothing is to abuse and exploit kids. But that's not exactly true, is it?

Primark makes an absolute fortune and could well afford decent working conditions for its employees without charging more for its goods. And firms that do treat their workers right could just as easily lower their prices and still make tidy sums.

But the way things are, cash is king and greedy company bosses are completely obsessed with making big bucks – either by mistreating employees or by hitting customers hard by cynically hiking up product costs to protect huge profit margins!

Primark is great for shoppers and should continue trading - with certain conditions.

Our government, so keen to bully and control others, should bloody well step in with legislation to stop such blatant abuses by cold-hearted capitalists who either callously exploit workers or charge extortionate prices for their goods or services.

But of course it won't because both scenarios so perfectly reflect its own cash-crazy, stuff the people attitude.

Current news reports include a shocking story of a teacher being stabbed to death in front of pupils at a school in Leeds.

Emotional tributes have been paid to Anne Maguire, 61, who was said to be a lovely lady adored by staff and scholars. A 15-year-old boy is in custody, being questioned.

Violence continues to rock the Ukraine, 30 people have died in a suicide bomber's attack on a political rally in Iraq: and 12 were killed and dozens wounded in a mortar assault in Damascus, Syria.  Misery piles upon misery it seems.

**April 30** – Pneumonia has clamed the life of popular film and TV star Bob Hoskins at the age of 71.

He's internationally known for starring in hit movies including Who Framed Roger Rabbit? Mona Lisa, Mermaids, Hook and the Long Good Friday.

His small screen credits include the classic series Pennies from Heaven plus Play for Today, On the Move, Van der Valk and BBC drama The Street.

**May 1** – Another birthday in Sam's household – this time it's her daughter Bec's 18th.  I'm going to the Bell this evening for a get-together to mark the occasion.

It's just been announced in the media that heroin is likely to have featured in the death of TV presenter Peaches Geldof.

The results of a toxicology report showed that the 25-year-old, who died suddenly last month, had the drug in her system, a brief inquest hearing was told this morning.

The proceedings were adjourned pending a fuller inquest to be held in July.

Peaches was the second daughter of musician and campaigner Bob Geldof and the late Paula Yates, who died of a heroin overdose at the age of 41.

**May 1 – a few hours later** – I saw something on Facebook earlier today that was both interesting and alarming.

It was a status put up by a friend of mine. The gist of it was "don't call me a racist just because I oppose the concept of my country being run according to a brutal enforcement of extreme Islamic law."

It went on to point out, quite rightly, that terms like Islam and Muslim referred to a religion, not a race. I totally agree - I've used the same argument about Jews and Judaism for a long time.

My friend, and others who think that way, may or may not be racists. But they are certainly bigots. And I find that equally disturbing.

And unfortunately far too many people continue to confuse race and religion, thinking Muslims are by definition from abroad whereas many will have actually been born here, making them English.

The really ignorant will view anyone with a brown complexion as an alien, totally disregarding nationality. Or they'll carelessly lump Muslims in with Poles and Romanians as unwanted outsiders.

Certain politicians seem happy to let this happen – encourage it, even.  And I find that despicable.

I share my friend's deep concern at the prospect of my country being run according to extremist rules and dogma, but I feel this applies just as much to other fanatical religious and political systems.

There are millions of devout Muslims whose philosophy is one of tolerance and respect.  Only a hard core minority wants a violent takeover bringing iron-fist enforcement of extreme doctrines.

There are similarly millions of moderate adherents to Judaism and Christianity just as repelled by the fanatical fringes of their own faiths.

I guess it gets back to Cameron's pointed comment about Britain being proud of its Christian heritage and Blair's inflammatory warning over fanatical Muslims.

And let's not forget that England's history is already blighted by brutal persecution and the ruthless enforcement of rigid, dogmatic forms of Christianity. I want a return to that just as much as I desire a switch to radical Islam – not at all. No sodding way!

We are a multicultural society. Why, oh why can't the moderate majorities of all religions club together and tell these hard line hate peddlers to bugger off?

I fear the answer is that twisted individuals with vested interests and suspect agendas on all sides are doing such a grand job in spreading anxiety, deepening the splits in communities for their own warped reasons.

**May 2** – Bec's birthday bash in the pub was a good one. Proud mum Sam was there, plus Bec's brother Alex and their dad Russell, close family friend Ian "Enoch" Dunn, Tina Mcauley, Alex's girlfriend Charley Hanks, Kelly Adams, Ryan Millen, Sharon Pendleton and Rich Jeffrey.

Several of Bec's female pals also turned up and I think the younger set hit Bournemouth's late night spots as the old fogeys like me headed for home.

Alex kindly offered to walk me from the pub to my own door to ensure I got back okay - and when I said no thanks I'd be fine, he insisted we swapped mobile phone numbers, saying: "Any time mate, day or night – if you need me, I'll be there."

Wow, I've misted over just writing that bit down. Sam and Russ, you've done a great job guys – this amazingly thoughtful young man is a credit to you both.

So is Bec, who couldn't stop thanking me for the card I'd given her and the money I'd put in it. Politeness, manners and showing respect cost nothing but are priceless to the recipient.

If you want to know how well someone's done as a parent, spend half an hour with their kids. Alex and Bec have turned out just fine. No doubt Rudy and Bailey will too – both are already well on their way, young as they are.

Apart from Bec's birthday gathering, I got to meet several other familiar faces at the pub including Jem Hannen, his nephew Jim, Chris Davis (as in Chris and Lou) and a guy called

Laurence (Lawrence?) who I hadn't seen for a while.

I also saw Becky Browning, a friend and barmaid at the Bell, who was celebrating her own birthday with her mates.

Carl stayed in to look after Rudy and Bailey, his and Sam's little sons. It's so nice to see a bloke willing to do this so his partner can go out to celebrate her daughter's 18th.

**May 3** – Max Clifford's been sent to jail for eight years. He was unrepentant and refused to apologise for indecent assaults on women and girls he continued to deny he'd committed. The judge said he'd shown a contemptuous attitude in court.

I guess this is why I take a rare wicked glee in Clifford's fate. People like him are not only contemptuous, they're contemptible. They persecute others, try to hide their own faults and don't care whose lives they wreck with their media-based meddling.

His speciality was "kiss and tell" scandals. Sounds like he should have stuck to kissing - and cuddling - the right people himself!

I usually warn against being too judgemental of others. None of us is perfect, no-one's entirely blameless, and we've all behaved very badly and deeply regrettably towards others at one time or another.

The ways we've done this vary from the irritating to the hurtful, the spiteful to the seriously damaging. Anyone who denies this is a deluded self-righteous fool.

But most of us aren't arrogant or stupid enough to make a habit of spotlighting others' faults when we have plenty of our own.

Don't chuck stones at others if you live in a glass house, like Maxie boy seems to have done. I guess that's the bottom line of what I'm saying.

Okay, fair enough, before anyone points out the obvious – yes, I was for many years a journalist myself; employed to report all aspects of life – its joy, its tragedy, even its seedier side. I used to cover magistrates' hearings.

But, in my own defence, when I did any story, court case or otherwise, I'd try to give a balanced account of both sides - unless I got the frustrating "no comment" which meant people denied themselves the chance to give their own version of events.

My introductory paragraphs would contain whichever seemed the most interesting aspect of the story. That was the way the job was taught at college and that was the way my own inbuilt instinct for fair play dictated I always attempted to do it.

I was livid when some of my reports were chopped and changed by sub-editors to give a twisted version of what I'd written. When I became a sub myself, I tried hard not to do this.

This meant I was frequently crossing swords with news editors and chief subs who wanted me to "spice things up."

I never was an ambulance-chaser, I resented the fact-manipulation and exaggeration that went on and hated all the expose-type stuff dishing the dirt.

Sure, some people deserved it – corrupt councillors, callous company bosses and so on – but I never wanted to be part of that side of the profession. I loved the feel-good and fun stuff and tried to avoid the hard news and muck-raking.

As a writer, that was one of the few bread-and-butter jobs I could do.

Certainly, if a local councillor was caught stealing from public funds or taking back-handers for supporting dodgy planning applications, they were fair game. But I still preferred that someone else wrote that story, not me.

I felt very uncomfortable when asked and still tried to be fair and balanced in my reporting.

But a mayor sleeping with his secretary behind his wife's back wasn't a news story in my view. That was a private matter, to be dealt with privately.

I never accepted the daft idea that community leaders had to be exemplary, whiter-than-white. As long as they did their jobs properly, serving the people, that's what mattered. Their private lives were their own business – unless they were criminals.

And the media obsession with sex scandals has always repelled me because it stops real issues being covered in any depth with any balance.

But glory-hunting, arrogant, holier-than-thou hypocrites take a different view – one that's unfortunately rife in media circles.

It's along the lines of – sod factual accuracy and the really important stuff; we want gross exaggeration, judgemental witch-hunts, sleaze and titillation!

Why? - Because that's what our readers demand! No, it's not; it's what you give them, time and time again. They don't really have a choice in the matter.

Well, they do – but only regarding which newspaper to buy. But that's no choice at all when the tabloids are all as bad as each other and busy people don't have the time to read bulkier publications with more balanced reports or sit and watch the TV news.

If you want to know why people really buy papers, cock up the crossword, lottery results or star signs, print the wrong chemist's rota or weather forecast, drop the sports pages or spell the bride's name wrong in a wedding report. Your switchboard will be jammed!

**May 4** – May the fourth be with you.  Sorry, couldn't resist that one as it's apparently Star Wars Day.

I find it quite amusing, but kind of appropriate, that Jedi is now accepted as a religion. If Star Wars fans live by Jedi principles, promoting the force of light and avoiding the dark side, that's a good thing, isn't it?

Speaking of religion, today's also been the day we've learned that the Archbishop of Canterbury, Justin Welby, has predictably joined in the "Christian country" debate following Cameron's recent provocative statement.

The leading clergyman accepted the danger of fundamentalism but still backed single-faith schools, saying they catered for some of the nation's poorest children.

He asserted that Church of England classrooms continued to "love and serve" communities as they had done for centuries. He felt the UK was "a deeply Christian country."

Well apart from making the same mistake as the Prime Minister in seeing the separate but closely allied countries in the UK as one, he's perfectly entitled to say what he did and defend and sell his own religious organisation.

As its top guy, it would be strange if he didn't. Depending on the careful phrasing of his comments – hopefully not being too inflammatory or divisive – he most certainly should be speaking on behalf of millions of his fellow believers in England and beyond.

Unlike Cameron, who should have kept his mouth shut and his nose out of religious issues. I'd have thought he had enough on his plate in the world of politics without meddling in areas beyond his mandate.

But he's always doing it. He must really love the sound of his own voice!

Other clergymen have chipped in with their views over the last few days, with former Archbishop of Canterbury Lord Williams saying that Anglicans and Roman Catholics should not be scared to practice their beliefs in multi-faith, "post Christian" Britain.

I agree – no-one should feel intimidated or dissuaded from declaring and following their own religion, whatever it is. Just so long as the way they do it doesn't impinge on someone else's right to do the same.

Agnostics, atheists, theosophists and humanists also have their places in a multi-faceted 21st-century community. Live and let live, don't be too gung-ho about it and respect others' different beliefs and views, I say.

And it's not escaped my notice that I'm saying it during the annual bank holiday weekend marking May Day.

This has taken on a very political significance in more recent times but its roots lie in the ancient pagan festival of Beltane. It's a sacred and profound occasion for Wiccans, Druids and the followers of other nature-based faiths.

Let's not forget them, or Buddhists, Jews, Hindus, Muslims, or adherents of any spiritual path for that matter. There's room for us all and no need to fight.

Tolerance and acceptance of different views are both desperately needed here – not religious bigotry or hate-laced fundamentalism seriously aggravated by inflammatory statements from politicians who should stay silent on such matters.

It's gone beyond ridiculous when people are told off for wearing religious symbols, such as Christian crosses on necklaces, at work.

Unless, of course, they're in a job where it could become a health and safety issue – for example, if they're called upon to operate certain types of machinery.

(Incidentally, the same total absence of respect and common sense exists over the wearing of non-religious stuff too, such as Remembrance poppies and Help for Heroes tee shirts).

There's hot debate at the moment over the burqa, an item of clothing worn by some Muslim women that conceals everything but their eyes.

I say some because there even seems to be disagreement among followers of the faith themselves over whether their holy book, the Quran, demands quite such a strict interpretation of what it says about women – and men - dressing modestly.

Some hard line sections of the Muslim community insist upon a burqa, other more liberal ones allow females to show their faces so long as they wear headscarves.

It's a very emotive issue. And for a lot of us, it's true that only seeing someone's eyes when we're so used to having a lot more on show can be quite shocking.

I'm not talking bikinis and swimming trunks here - just normal clothing frequently worn in public, such as knee-length skirts and short-sleeved shirts.

It's very difficult to avoid immediately associating the burqa with the concept of shady people with something to hide. After all, criminals often wear masks and hoods. So do terrorists, violent thugs and nasty troublemakers of all kinds.

I'm not saying this is the right way of thinking and I certainly mean no offence on such a highly controversial subject.  But it's true that, no doubt wrongly, this mindset is deeply ingrained in our collective consciousness.  It's been there for ages.

And, just like the Christian cross, there are certain situations where a burqa would be totally unsuitable – even hazardous for the wearer.

Other countries have strict rules governing clothing and their inhabitants would be outraged to come here and see so much bare flesh on display.

We, in turn, would be just as startled by some of the stringent dress rules, alcohol bans and other unfamiliar customs on visiting other lands.

Variety is the spice of life, they say, and England – Britain, even – is a place where far more liberal attitudes prevail on all sorts of matters. There is no right or wrong here, just different ways of looking at things.

Time for a lot more sensitivity, understanding, mutual respect and common sense, methinks!

**May 6** – Well, it's the Tuesday after a bank holiday weekend and for many it means back to the grind after three days of fun and frivolity.

Helping people return to Earth with a massive crash is our compassionate, caring government with its announcement today that a jobless person's benefits will be axed if they refuse to take one of the notorious zero-hours contract positions on offer.

Talk about kicking folk when they're down! This is a double blow because those taking such jobs are already judged to be in full-time employment, therefore denied any welfare payments from the state.

This in itself is an absolute disgrace because under such contracts employees are no longer guaranteed either work or payment – leaving them at the mercy of bosses with no obligation or motivation to make sure they can survive financially.

Apparently there are a million or so zero-hours contract workers in the UK. These people are little more than slaves at the mercy of unscrupulous capitalists.

The fact that they have no workers' rights is deplorable in itself.

Some, probably a small minority, might be willing to handle all this uncertainty and take such jobs – namely those simply topping up the main household income.

But many others, probably the vast majority, will be needing and seeking employment that pays the bills.

So they wouldn't entertain a risky zero-hours deal unless they were really desperate. Sadly, a growing number are.

Work or no work, they still have to find the rent plus cash for food and other essentials. No wages and denial of welfare means they're expected to find these funds out of thin air. How cruel and insane is that?

It places citizens in a perilous situation. Flipping 'eck - even kids in Indian "concentration camp" sweat shops apparently receive 60p a day. English folk on these despicable contracts aren't even assured of getting that!

All this is disgusting enough, but to then get Cameron and crew really twisting the knife by forcing the unemployed to take such positions truly is beyond the pale.

Accept the job with no guarantee of work or wages, or don't take it and lose out on benefit payments. Some choice! Who the hell do these cruel crazies think they are?

One of the reasons unemployment looks like its falling is the massive number of people on these God-awful contracts. Devious figure massaging is another.

What's really sickening is the fact that all this comes as these callous, bonkers, aloof, totally out of touch politicians persist in repeating the blatant lie that our economy is growing and confidence is also on the up.

Not round these parts, mate!  No-one I know is all that confident.  Most are cash-strapped and wary over where the axe will fall next.

Nervous bosses are cutting jobs and hours, benefit claimants are suffering withdrawal of payments and there's financial strife, closures, service breakdowns and growing anxiety wherever you look.

Jobcentre staff are told to turn up the heat– insanely ordering clients to sign on daily or do community tasks to keep getting their benefits - or go on useless training courses, temporary placements or zero-hours contracts, none assuring paid work.

And all because there are so few genuine cash-for-labour positions available.  The days of full employment and job security are long gone.

Whole industries have collapsed and traditional work opportunities continue to disappear as the population grows apace.

More and more people are chasing a dwindling number of proper paid vacancies – and millions can't find lifetime careers, so spend some of their working years in employment, others reliant on benefits – constantly edgy, always in a state of flux.

But politicians ignore these stark realities in their doomed bid to run the country using dread and deception.

The whole sorry mess stinks to high heaven.  Thanks a lot

Dave, George and Nick - you're bleeding stars!

But before we lay all the blame at the coalition's door, let's take time out to remember Labour's part in all this.

The start of my own bitter battle with benefits officers actually dated back to the tail end of Gordon Brown's reign, before this mad bunch had the chance to inflict their wholesale damage. It just intensified under them.

Brown was already warning of his own welfare payments clampdown as we went to the polls - and I was caught as this began to take effect.

We all know what happened next – Labour lost the election and the Tories and Lib Dems seized power by default after joining forces to give them a combined majority.

In actual fact, our bizarre benefits system, defying all logic, consistency and common sense, is the handiwork of successive Labour and Tory governments over the decades.

But Dave, Georgie, Nicky boy and their coalition cut-throat clowns have taken unrealistic, unfeeling, unfathomable policy-making to a whole new level. Under them, it's become cold and brutal.

**May 7** – I watched The Hobbit Two – the Desolation of Smaug last night, having just bought it on DVD. And I thoroughly enjoyed it.

It will now go in my collection alongside the first Hobbit film, An Unexpected Journey, and the Lord of the Rings trilogy.

These star-studded blockbuster movies are a treat for all the family with great performances and terrific special effects. They really do justice to the wonderful imagination and mesmerising story-telling skills of original author J R R Tolkien.

Getting back to religious tolerance and common sense, I saw a great status on Facebook today. It took the mick brilliantly without being offensive.

It was announced in the news this week that the Subway sandwich takeaway shops chain has decided to stop selling ham and bacon as it could offend Muslims.

The humorous status, put up by a friend, said that following Subway's lead, B and Q hardware stores had stopped stocking wood and nails as it might offend Christians.

I don't think there's any truth in this second statement – yet!

My mate's Facebook funny, no doubt borrowed from someone else, was a fantastic way of ridiculing a daft situation that's really getting out of hand.

Lots of stuff sold in shops offends me. I just avoid those shops. Many programmes on TV get on my wick. So I don't watch them. Certain books, magazines and newspapers insult my sensibilities – so I don't read them.

And when it comes to clothing, we all have our personal choices and pet hates.

It's so damned simple – or at least should be!

Other people will buy, wear, eat, watch, read and listen differently and be put off by my preferences. We can disagree and still get on, for goodness' sake – it's hardly rocket science!

If a shop selling food – or anything else for that matter – upsets too many people and proves to be seriously unpopular, it will go out of business within a very short space of time.  A widely offensive TV show won't last long before producers pull the plug.

A universally hated CD, DVD or book will soon be taken off the shelves. And people won't download anything they don't like – or if they do by accident, they'll rapidly delete it.

Market forces and public opinion will ensure that anything that's really deeply offensive or insulting will be jettisoned pretty frigging sharpish without the need for an over-the-top enforcement of yet more silly rules and restrictions.

Yet power-mad PC (politically correct) extremists seem determined to control every aspect of our lives.  It's very annoying and actually quite sinister.

*************************************

# CHAPTER THREE – MIXED MESSAGES

**May 7 – a few hours later** - Reading through older parts of my on-going life journal can be quite interesting for me.  It provides me with a chance to see in black and white how my views have changed significantly in some respects but in others remained much the same.

I also realise that I keep on saying the same things but in slightly different ways – in between recording as-yet unmentioned cherished memories or relating and commenting on new personal experiences and events in the outside world.

Am I short-changing anyone daft enough to buy and read my paperbacks or get my written work through Kindle - by repeating what I've said before, albeit with an altered emphasis?  Maybe I am, but I don't intend to.

Sometimes it's worth repeating stuff when it's relevant to new developments – to emphasize points we're making.  Some things are worth saying – stressing even - time and time again if we think they're important enough.

Let's face it, we all do this in conversation, all the time – go over old ground.  We have our own favourite tales we keep recounting, we all like re-stating our pet views and opinions to others, and sometimes we simply forget what we have or haven't already told someone.

I just do it in written prose, that's all.  Well, that's my excuse and I'm sticking to it! The same applies to some of my lyrics too, as it happens.

**May 8** – Wishing a happy birthday to my brother-in-law, David Dixon, and my pal Linda Franceschi.

Linda's back home in Corsica now.  She and I became friends when she lived in Boscombe, worked at the Bell and became a great mate of Sam Excell's.

Linda's sister Flavie is also my friend and a few years ago I attended her wedding.  Flavie still lives in Boscombe and I see her about now and then.  I keep in touch with both of them via Facebook.

Following on from the Subway sandwich shops debate, we now have in today's news the allegation that top supermarkets like Tescos and Sainsburys are selling halal chicken and lamb without telling customers.

Halal meat is that from animals slaughtered under Islamic law by having their throats cut while they're still alive and aware. A prayer is said just before this happens.

It's claimed the meat is fresher and cleaner that way.

But the method raises animal welfare issues; with the RSPCA saying that it can cause unnecessary suffering, pain and distress – more so than if the creature's stunned before being killed.

I'm with the animal charity on this one – but then, I'm not a Muslim. If I was, I'd no doubt be a supporter of the halal method.

There's a similar debate over kosher food rules obeyed by Jews. Once again, there's no right or wrong, just different ways of doing things based on your religious beliefs.

My main concern over the supermarket meat issue is that shoppers aren't being told – just like with the horse meat in burgers furore of a short while ago.

There's nothing wrong with any of these meats. They're all perfectly edible. The real scandals in my eyes have been the high levels of deception involved.

Labelling food products to let customers know what exactly they're getting and how it's been brought from natural habitat to retail outlet is the obvious answer. They then have a choice over whether to buy and eat them or not.

People need to be supplied with all the relevant facts so they can make informed decisions they're comfortable with.

I don't think there's any coincidence that the Subway and supermarket controversies are hitting the headlines at much the same time.

Sure, food companies should be open and honest and not try to hide what they're up to. Consumers should be made fully aware of what's happening and why.

But I deeply suspect that underneath all the revelations and arguments lies a cold, calculated and concerted effort to demonize Muslims.

And that's part of a wider, increasingly dirty campaign to stir up suspicion and hatred between different ethical groups. I find this both very alarming and pretty damned chilling.

Elsewhere in the news, it's been announced that Barclays Bank is to cut 19,000 jobs – more than half of them in the UK. A recovering economy, growing confidence and more people in work eh, Davey boy? Ha! Ha! – Gotcha!

Okay, my laughter is sardonic, and in truth it's no joking matter – certainly not for the bank employees left jobless with slim chances of securing alternative paid work.

Or the millions of others on the scrapheap - either unemployed, doing short-term unpaid work, on training schemes or stuck on those terrible zero hours contracts.

With critical levels of job insecurity, benefit cuts, friction growing between our community's various sections and a media hell bent on deepening suspicion and division, it's hardly surprising people are so worried, edgy and fractious.

Especially when that same media seems determined to further scare us witless with wildly excessive stories including frenzied witch-hunts, doom-laden long term weather forecasts and brutal, incessant public health warnings.

Confidence has been shattered into tiny pieces and morale's hit rock bottom. No wonder they call it broken Britain.

It all seems so hopeless and struggling on starts to resemble a pointless waste of time and energy. But it really isn't – that's just the way it's painted thanks to our media's twisted, ugly version of reality and the politicians' deliberately mixed messages and exceedingly dubious assertions.

How stupid do they think we are? But they don't care – just so long as they spread falsehoods and confusion, keeping us anxious, uncertain of the truth and increasingly wary and resentful of each other while they stir us all up and stay in the driving seat.

There is good news – everywhere.  You just have to look for it. Just around the corner is a genuine story of courage or resilience, compassion or hope.  But these heart-warming tales are savagely shunted aside in the stampede to frighten and manipulate.

**May 10 – 6.30pm** – Today's been chuffing marvellous!  Why? – Because I went to my granddaughter Chloe's first birthday party in Ferndown.

It's actually her special day on Wednesday – the 14th – but proud parents Phil and Emily, my son and daughter-in-law, decided to hold the shindig today as it was more convenient for most people.

It was actually staged at Emily's parents' house, more spacious than Phil and Em's nearby flat.

So Em's mum and dad,  Gail and Keith Cooper were present, alongside Em's sister Rachel with baby daughter Lily, Em and Rachel's brother Simon, Chloe and her brothers Harvey and Lucas (both three), plus Phil's stepsister Ali, her fiancé Terry and their baby girl Roxanna.

Several of Phil and Emily's female friends also turned up, some with their kids, and my ex-wife Joe (Phil's mum) and her sister Cheryl attended too. Hamish the Cooper family dog and their pet cat added an animal element to the proceedings.

It was great seeing my grandchildren Chloe, Lucas and Harvey again and also meeting Roxanna and Lily for the first time.  The little ones were all really well-behaved and seemed to be having a lot of fun, which was very nice to see.

I got a taxi to the party and spent a lovely few hours with the family and their friends.  Phil kindly gave me a lift home as he had to drop Lucas back with mum Becky at West Howe – half the way between Ferndown and my place.

It was a relief that Keith could be there as he's only just returned home after 10 days in hospital with pneumonia.  Stuart – Joe's feller, Ali's dad and Phil's stepfather - couldn't make it as he was working until early evening.

Occasions like this are just plain wonderful – the icing on life's cake.  And an assortment of real cakes, including a special birthday chocolate sponge with one candle, featured heavily as part of a very pleasant finger buffet.

It was an absolutely super event destined to be a treasured memory for all involved.  And that's so cool!

**May 14** – And today's the day itself.  Happy first birthday Chloe, you precious girl, Granddad Martin is so, so proud of you!

Many happy returns also to my great mate Theresa Bevis, and to Carole Jones' daughter Leesa, too.  Celebrations all round it seems!

Well, it does in my little world – but not in the bigger, much crueler outside one, where at least 200 workers have died in a coal mine explosion in western Turkey.

And, much closer to home, brave 19-year-old Stephen Sutton, who raised millions of pounds for cancer sufferers, has finally lost his own battle with the dreadful disease.

Stephen, from Burntwood, Staffordshire, became an inspirational figure and a national hero as he told his story on social networking sites after being diagnosed with the killer condition at the age of 15.

He raised more than 3.2 million for the Teenage Cancer Trust as his good-natured and courageous posts became an internet sensation. RIP Stephen, you wonderful human being.

**May 15** – There have been more twists and turns in the Emmerdale story line about troubled teenager Belle Dingle. Basically, her family has used extreme shock tactics to persuade her to change her plea from guilty to not guilty pending her murder trial.

Now terrified at the prospect of prison, she's desperately looking for ways to avoid it if the jury don't believe that her friend Gemma's death was a tragic accident. Drunken Gemma sustained a fatal head injury after Belle angrily pushed her during a row.

So Belle's come up with the incredibly dumb idea that the court might take pity on her if she's pregnant. Her male friend Sean has eagerly agreed to help her with this and they're trying to get a quiet moment alone together so they can get jiggy. He's in love with her. She likes him too but she's more driven by desperation than romance.

But there's a massive flaw in her thinking and we can see her digging herself deeper and deeper into the mire. Why? – Because the main reason she and Gemma fell out was the fact that Sean, who both of them fancied, had got Gemma pregnant during a drunken fumble while supposedly Belle's boyfriend. Gemma later had an abortion.

If all this came out in court, as no doubt it would, Belle would look like a spiteful, vengeful young woman, incensed by her friend's traitorous actions, who'd do anything to have Sean all to herself and have her own baby with him – even kill Gemma to get her out of the way.

Up to now, Belle's always been portrayed as a very bright teenager. But her sharp perception has deserted her this time as her traumatised and confused mental state has led to an uncharacteristic bout of gross stupidity.

**May 16** – MPs are apparently worried about bullying in the Police Federation - the organisation representing rank-and-file coppers in England and Wales.

In a damning report, the Home Affairs Committee has called for an urgent reform of the federation to combat this.

If the allegation is true, this is a scandalous state of affairs needing swift action to stop such behaviour immediately.

But don't you think it's a bit rich that MPs are making this claim when their colleagues in the government are just as guilty of odious bullyboy tactics – probably more so?

This coalition has taken brutal treatment of citizens to a whole new level, using fiscal penalties and high-handed bureaucratic controls to metaphorically cosh people over the head and stab them in the face.

I hate bullies no matter where they operate – and these smart suited Whitehall thugs are among the worst of all. How dare they try to take the moral high ground when they perceive there's bullying elsewhere?!

Get your own house in order first, you horrible, hypocritical shower!

**May 17** – Today is my beloved big sister Jan's birthday so I'm having an alcohol-free day in her honour while remembering her.

The kind, lovely, brilliant woman who made a dream come true for me never touched a drop in her whole life. She died two years ago, aged 68. I've lit a candle for her.

**May 18** – The gap between obscene wealth and critical poverty in our troubled country is wider than ever, according to the annual rich list published today.

Millions suffering under the coalition's unfair and unnecessary austerity policies will no doubt be delighted to learn that other lucky gits are better off than ever. It's nothing short of a disgrace!

But I guess we shouldn't be too surprised – certain individuals (many of them politicians) will prosper while others struggle financially no matter who's in power.

The Tories are just more honest about their "we're rich, sod you lot" attitude.

People making money – even millions of pounds – isn't the issue for me. It's when the figures ridiculously reach into the billions while others suffer extreme fiscal hardship that I start having a real problem with it.

Especially when Cameron and crew – and particularly the traitorous Clegg – really rub salt in the wounds by pandering to the loaded while penalising the poor.

Bloody hell – live in luxury by all means but give some to your riches to help the less fortunate, because no-one needs that much!

**May 21, 6pm** – I've been buying some more great music on CDs. Earlier today, I picked up second-hand copies of albums by Neil Young, Cat Stevens, Bruce Springsteen, Nirvana, Radiohead and Ultravox.

A few weeks ago, I secured CDs by Girlschool, Alice Cooper, Rainbow, Saxon, the Faces and Gary Numan. Altogether, a bit of a varied assortment, as usual.

**May 22** – It's exactly a year ago today, date-wise, that I received my first paperback copies of Sunshine and Ice Volume One through the post. It was on general release within a fortnight and put out on Kindle a few weeks later.

Since then, Volumes Two to Six have also been published and the seventh is about to be. It's being printed up as I write. I still await my first royalty cheque.

A friend of mine with all six published paperbacks sent me a Facebook message last week saying he'd just started Volume Four – Rosebeds and Dustbins/Snow and Hatred. I replied that I was chuffed he was still reading them.

Perhaps he's writing a thesis on mental instability and how one person can so easily descend into madness as life unfolds, things happen and years pass!

Today being polling day, I went to a local church hall this morning to vote for the Green Party in the European elections.

Some areas of the country also have local council elections, but not here.

I sincerely hope that other people either vote Green or Labour to give our dreadful coalition government a well-deserved bloody nose.

But I fear that in fact many will be voting for UKIP, the BNP and other anti-Europe, foreigner-wary parties demanding stringent immigration rules as part of a thinly-disguised bigot's agenda.

And come next May's general election, it will be interesting to see if those using their vote today to protest against the main parties' pro-Europe attitudes and muddled immigration policies have actually given up on the big three for good or decide to return meekly to their traditional folds having made their point.

I'd actually much rather see this than an alarming growth in support for dangerous people with ugly, intolerant and highly divisive hate-laced agendas deceptively couched in very reasonable, apparently straight-talking language.

Ideally I'd love more folk to back the Greens at all elections. But it's an uphill struggle and I fully accept that this is a lot more likely to happen in Europe, where they are a heck of a lot stronger – a real force to be reckoned with.

Sadly, many people don't even bother to vote these days because they're so bitterly disillusioned with politicians as a breed and their frequently broken promises.

Some feel strongly that it makes no difference whether they go to the polls or not - nothing will change because the system's rigged to maintain the flawed status quo.

I fully understand and have a lot of sympathy for both views - but I still feel that those who waste the vote others have fought bravely to secure for them can't really moan too loudly when governments come up with policies and decisions they don't like.

**May 23**   Nigel Farage and his United Kingdom Independence Party are celebrating today after making the significant inroads in the local authority elections that many had predicted, others had hoped for and I'd feared.

Okay, so UKIP didn't win control of any councils, but then they weren't expecting to. They did, however, secure 25 per cent of the total votes cast and won scores of seats.

Results are still coming in but so far it's clear that Labour's done well while the Conservatives have suffered big losses and the Liberal Democrats have taken a right pasting.

With 69 councils declared, Labour has gained 113 seats, UKIP 89; the Lib Dems lost 104 and the Conservatives, 103.  The Green Party has more than doubled its seat tally already - from four to nine. Cool!

While Farage and Labour leader Ed Miliband smile, the Tories and Lib Dems are being typically bullish, playing down their defeats and asserting that come the general election, it will be a different story.

They might be right – but this sort of stubborn arrogance annoys me intensely.  The voters have given these guys a clear message that they're unhappy with the way they're running our country.  They should ruddy well take heed. But they won't.

Even last night, with only one council declared – Sunderland, gained by Labour – nervous Tories were already talking about striking a deal with UKIP in a bid to keep the reds out of power.

So they're quite happy to ditch the largely discredited Lib Dems and climb into bed with Farage and co in a desperate bid to block Labour, keep control and carry on running – and ruining - our country with no clear mandate to do so!  Nice people!

UKIP leaders were having none of it, saying the public are turning to them because they're a fresh, honest, straight-talking alternative, not part of the tired, deceptive, unreliable old guard.

Elsewhere in the news, it's been announced that Dutchman Louis van Gaal will be Manchester United's new manager from next season onwards on a three-year contract.  Ryan Giggs will be his second-in-command.

Currently in charge of the Netherlands' national team for the fast-approaching World Cup tournament in Brazil, van Gaal, 62, is a skilled and highly-respected manager who's won trophies with teams in Holland, Spain and Germany.  I wish him well at Old Trafford.

While writing this, I've been playing a couple of Cat Stevens CDs.  What a talent!  – A musician and poet of the highest order. He made great albums and some of his most famous songs have been widely used by others (Wild World, Father and Son, Here Comes My Baby and the First Cut is the Deepest, for example).

**May 24** – Today would have been my 28th wedding anniversary. The marriage lasted seven years. Cest la vie.

Update on the local authority elections - with 148 councils declared and 13 still to go, the Lib Dems have lost 273 seats and the Conservatives 188.

Labour has gained 275, but the real success story has indeed been UKIP, rocketing from just two seats to 155.

Labour will rule 75 councils (+6), the Tories 39 (-11), the Lib Dems 6 (-2) and UKIP none. No party has overall control of 28 authorities (+7).

Delighted Nigel Farage says his UKIP party has become a real force to be reckoned with overnight; while Labour leaders are apparently a tad disappointed their party didn't do slightly better.

Now we await the results of the European elections, due to be announced late tomorrow (Sunday) and Monday.

In the meantime, I shall leave commenting on issues in the outside world briefly to return to matters in my own little corner of existence.

You know, I could kick myself sometimes. The other day I was chatting to a friend about a mutual pal and, to be honest, it got a bit bitchy.

The person under discussion is actually a very good friend of both of us. I have a lot of time for them and I think the mate I was talking to has too.

I didn't intend my sarcastic but light-hearted comments to be taken too seriously.  But in retrospect I'm more than a bit angry with myself for taking such unnecessary cheap shots at someone I actually like – just to show off my acerbic wit.

Note to self – it ain't big, it ain't clever.  You like this individual so why do it, you fool?

**May 26** – History's been made this weekend.  It's the first time since 1910 that a political party other than Labour or the Conservatives has won a nationwide election.

I find it both worrying and ironic that the anti-Europe UKIP party has topped the poll in Britain's section of the European elections.

UKIP has clinched 24 seats in the Euro parliament, racking up 28 per cent of the vote.  Labour secured 20 seats (25%), the Conservatives 19 (24%) and the Green Party three (8%).  Once again the biggest losers were the Liberal Democrats, slipping to fifth and retaining only one of the 11 seats they started with (7%).

With more results due in throughout today, it's a situation that's being mirrored in other countries where nationalistic, Euro-sceptic parties have given the more moderate democrats, socialists and conservatives a good old bashing.

France's right-wing national front has swept to victory and the message across the continent is clear - communities in various countries are fed up with the onward march of the monolithic

European super-state and desire a swift reversal of open-border immigration policies and the re-assertion of national identities.

Will the politicians listen?  They'd be mad not to.  But then, they are a pretty unhinged lot, aren't they?

Nick Clegg's position as Lib Dem leader and deputy prime minister is looking increasingly untenable.  Serves him right!

Well, it being a bank holiday weekend, I popped along to the Bell (Seabourne's) last night (Sunday) to sup pints, chat with mates and enjoy live music courtesy of soul singer Alexander.

I hooked up with John Gaynor, Mark Hemington, Bev Jones, Stu and Melody Moss, Matt Brandt, Dani Knight, Rebecca Browning, Clare Hayes and a mate called Jim – don't know his surname.

Stu, who possesses signed copies of all six of my published paperbacks, was very kind about my skills as a writer.  I gave him the books after he expressed an interest in them.

And I had a pleasant but brief trip down Memory Lane with Bev, who was updating me on mutual friends who were once part of our crazy "Tuesday night club" wine, chat and laughter sessions at her old flat in Boscombe a few years ago.

I got home from the pub in time to tune in to BBC Three's TV coverage of Katy Perry's bill-topping performance at Radio One's Big Weekend festival in Glasgow.  I like Katy's music anyway but this set showed just how well she can cut it live.

Fluorescent costumes and big-screen displays enhanced the songs and the show ended with her smash hit Firework – accompanied by a spectacular firework display.  Cool!

**May 27** – I've just been playing Cat Stevens' album Tea for the Tillerman for the second time since securing it on second-hand CD last week.

And once again I've come under the spell of this brilliant musical treat, which I first heard and fell in love with just after its release in 1970.  Its decades since I heard it all the way through.

The melodies are great, the lyrics even better.  I'd forgotten just how good Mr Stevens was as a singer-songwriter – right up there with the best.

(He now calls himself Yusuf Islam, having converted to that religion. And he's as well known these days for his work as a humanitarian, peace campaigner and philanthropist).

It was a regrettable oversight that I omitted this mighty fine album from my top fifty all-time favourites, as written down in my last book, Persistent Illusions.

But then, I also missed out Hunky Dory, Making Movies, Screamadelica, Rumours, What's Going On?, New Boots and Panties, Houses of the Holy, Let it Bleed, Electric Ladyland, the Queen is Dead and A Trick of the Tail – to name just a few.

I left Cat Stevens out of my top 20 solo male performers, along with Donovan, Michael Jackson, Peter Gabriel, Prince and, amazingly, Bob Dylan! Oops! And Katy Perry, Carole King, Carly Simon and Dolly Parton were missing from my female list.

I further realised afterwards that I'd not included the Eagles, the Cure, the Kinks, the Undertones, King Crimson, Thin Lizzy, the Faces, Simple Minds, Free, Metallica, the Electric Light Orchestra or Joy Division in my run-down of my 30 top bands.

Just goes to show how tricky it can get when you try to compile summaries of your favourites – especially, I find, where music is concerned.  Humble apologies to all those I overlooked.

Talking about being overlooked, it seems politicians all over Europe have totally failed to notice the depth of feeling among voters seriously unhappy about the relentless enforcement of the oppressive, monolithic super-state.

Citizens throughout the continent chose Euro-sceptic, nationalistic parties in their millions at the weekend's poll for the European Parliament.

This sent shock waves rippling across the borders, reflected in UKIP's triumph on our own island.

Cameron has started talking of dramatically reforming the European Union from the inside and holding a UK referendum to see if we want to stay in or leave the union.

But you know damned well it's nowhere near that simple, Dave – no matter how hard UKIP supremo Nigel Farage tries to imply that it is.

I was studying economics at school in the run-up to our joining the old Common Market, as it was then called, in 1971.  As an exercise, our teacher got us to look at the pros and cons of our jumping on board.

We concluded – rightly, in our teacher's view – that, measured over the next five years, the advantages and disadvantages would balance each other out.

But that was 40 years ago and since then we've signed treaty after treaty further entangling us in the fast-growing Euro spider web.

Meanwhile, that web has solidified and mutated from a relatively loose and very beneficial trading agreement – a good idea - into an iron framework of political might, rigid bureaucracy and brutal law enforcement – an oppressive nightmare.

But this, of course, is where the real power brokers, those in the shadows pulling the strings of their political lackeys and scapegoats, were heading all along. I fear it's a bit late in the day to try and extricate ourselves now.

We'd have to forcibly pull ourselves out altogether – which could spell economic and political suicide. We should have stood our ground decades ago – or not signed up in the first place. But, as I said, that wasn't part of the plan.

That's why successive Labour and Tory government ministers have consistently been pro-EU. Except Thatcher, that is – she tried to stand up against Europe and the next we knew she was out on her ear.

This is where Farage and co have been more than a bit deceptive in suggesting it would be easy to back out of the EU. It wouldn't. The ramifications could be immense.

It will be very interesting to see how the UKIP representatives get on when they take their seats in the European Parliament.

As for Cameron and his cynical new enthusiasm for a referendum, he, too, is fully aware that disengaging from the union would be a far from straightforward matter and it would make little difference whether we held a nationwide one-issue poll or not.

**May 29** – Re-acquainting myself with the beautiful words and music of Cat Stevens has led me to investigate why he converted from Christianity to Islam and what he's been up to since leaving behind his pop star persona.

And I discovered that Cat – or Yusuf as he now prefers – is a deeply spiritual man who's used his fame and energy to set up charities, spearhead humanitarian causes and spread a message of peace and tolerance across the world.

In short, hc's my kind of Muslim – thc right kind, cnhancing the positive vibration. Just like George Harrison was my kind of Krishna follower, Bob Marley my sort of Rastafarian, Pete Townsend is my kind of Meher Baba advocate, Tina Turner's my kind of Buddhist, Bob Dylan my sort of Jew and Alice Cooper, my kind of Christian.

You know, talented celebrities who believe you can have a lot of fun sharing your gift with the world, spreading joy and strengthening that positive vibe, entertaining people and maybe doing good deeds as well – respecting your chosen faith without ramming it down others' throats.

Then we have the politicians like Nick Clegg. The Lib Dem knives are out following the party's disastrous but totally predictable fall from grace at the local and Euro elections.

There are calls for him to go – but he was on the news today refusing to budge. Looks like he's going to have to be forcibly ousted as he ain't going either willingly or quietly.

Elsewhere in the news, Manchester United's former chief executive Malcolm Glazer has died, aged 85.

The American billionaire and his family purchased United for £790m in May 2005 amid protests from the Premier League club's fans.

But the players went on to win five Premier League titles and the Champions League under the Glazers' ownership.

New Yorker Malcolm's sons, Joel and Avram, took over the day-to-day running of the club in April 2006 after their father suffered a stroke.

The Glazer family retains a 90 per cent share in United and a press statement today said the death of its patriarch would not affect the club's standing as a world-famous brand.

BRAND? It's a frigging football team! Nike, Umbro and Puma are brands. United is a global sporting phenomenon that has sold shed loads of merchandise due to its continued success on the field of play. Get it right, knuckleheads!

But then, I've noticed this quite a lot lately. Pop stars are also being called brands. And, back in 2012 when we hosted the summer Olympic Games, I believe even the word "Olympics" and the distinctive traditional five rings symbol were patented.

I suppose we shouldn't be too surprised, because in truth Britain is no longer an alliance of countries – it's a corporation, and has been for many moons.

Yes, a company, a brand, being run just like a business by hard-nosed capitalists obsessed with profit and loss who use the rest of us as little more than insignificant worker bees. The same is true of America, and no doubt other so-called countries too.

Our national flags are our logos - that's all. And Scotland's independence debate and forthcoming referendum centre on a bid to form a break-away firm.

Welcome to the 21<sup>st</sup> century!

But I'll still persist in the old-fashioned mode of thinking that England is my beloved homeland. I hope others do too – but without being jingoistic, racist or bigoted.

**May 29 – evening** – I was watching an old episode of that Jeremy Kyle show on TV this afternoon. And two thoughts occurred to me.

The first was his incredible hypocrisy. He's always slating Facebook, saying he doesn't understand it and hates it with a passion.

Yet as we returned to the programme after an ad break, there was a short segment revealing that the show's joined the social networking site and proudly declares that it's had a million "likes" so far!

This is so amazingly and blatantly two-faced it actually beggars belief!

My second thought was instigated by the Kyle team's apparent obsession with what they term "conflict and resolution."

This sounds very trendy and American to me. Basically, it works on the theory that the only effective way to cure ills and resolve disputes is by first bringing all the hurt and rage to the surface – often involving bitter outburst and violent confrontations.

That's the sole sure-fire method of making people face up to their problems, unblock communication channels, diffuse situations and heal emotional wounds, it's said.

By then acknowledging, accepting and clearing up the resultant ugly mess, they can finally totally move on and progress towards closure and harmony, some assert.

That's the theory, anyway. But I'm far from convinced. Sure, this might well work in certain cases and circumstances. But in others, dredging up highly corrosive muck from the past could do a heck of a lot more harm than good.

Old wounds could be re-opened and very painful memories brought back into the sharpest focus, causing untold damage and misery.

Crucial factors would be how long ago the troubles occurred, how serious the impact was and how successful the people have been in moving on. If they haven't at all, and their lives remain severely blighted, then the Kyle team's method could work.

But if the rage and hurt have been largely left behind in the past and the emotional injuries pretty much healed, is it really very wise to force folk to take a deeply disturbing and potentially lethal trip down Memory Lane? I would say probably not.

That's what I think, anyway.

**May 30** – Today's the day of Stephen Sutton's funeral. Diagnosed with terminal cancer at 15, he spent the last four years of his short life becoming an internet phenomenon by teaching people how to face hardship with grace and humour.

Rather than feel sorry for himself, he used his predicament to inspire others and raised millions of pounds for charities set up to help fellow sufferers.

His positive response to the worst news possible has been a shining example of how incredible human beings can be. I'm welling up writing this.

Thumbs up to you, Steve. What a guy! You didn't live long, but boy what an impact you made - for all the right reasons. Rest in peace feller – your work is done and your memory will live on. What a brilliant legacy.

****************************************

# CHAPTER FOUR – ENDLESS SPIRAL

**May 31** – I went round Sam and Carl's yesterday and spent a highly enjoyable few hours with them, Bec, Rudy, Bailey, the family's pet dogs Blaze and Albert, Tina Mcauley, Russell, Jimmy and his daughter Molly. Sweet!

But to briefly get a tad philosophical, it's often said that two wrongs don't make a right. I agree.

Hitting back, fighting fire with fire and inflicting as much damage on others as they have on you or yours might well release pent-up anger and make you feel good – fleetingly.

But it makes you no better than those who have caused you pain.

No, the correct course of action is to rise above ugly wrongdoing and keep your own behaviour virtuous by comparison.

This is far easier said than done, of course, but we sure must try – otherwise we just perpetuate an endless spiral of tit-for-tat hurt and heartache.

Everyone suffers – you included. And that's just crazy.

Let forgiveness put a stop to the misery and douse the flames of rage and resentment - for all our sakes. Or at least give it a go. The results could be amazing.

**June 2** – Yesterday, a Sunday, was a very satisfactory one for yours truly. First off, I renewed contact with an old pal via Facebook. Then, I had a pleasant couple of hours in my local pub.

Getting home from there, I sat down just in time to enjoy a terrific television treat. Please allow me to explain.

You might remember me referring to Andy Bethune earlier in this book as one of my former drinking buddies in the pubs and social clubs around Southbourne and Boscombe. He was one of the new-wave Teddy boys I met through Tom Jones.

I didn't realise Andy was on Facebook until by chance I saw the name Slick Bethune on another mate's friends list. I didn't recognise the nickname – he didn't use it when we hung out together – but it's quite an unusual surname so I looked up his FB page and discovered that yes indeed this was my old mucker.

I immediately sent him a friend request and switched on my computer this morning to find that he'd accepted me. So that's Andy, Steve Gray, Christine Jones and Carole Jones from the old gang I'm now back in contact with on FB.

Chris and Tom's daughter Samantha is also a Facebook friend and of course I'm also in touch with my bro Tom himself again by mobile phone (it appears he's not on FB).

I think it's so damned appropriate that I'm now re-united with some of my old mates from those fun-filled Home Guard days thanks to Sam Excell, who persuaded me to join the social networking site.

I've already explained that Sam, then a teenager, used to baby-sit for Tom and Chris. Her parents were Home Guard stalwarts and her uncle "Cess" used to run the bar.

Slick, or Andy as I knew him, was a sterling booze brother and I have many fond memories of our times with the old gang in the local clubs and pubs.

One abiding recollection I have is of the time he and I, along with Christine and my then wife Joe, accompanied Tom when he was booked to put on a New Year disco show in Poole. I think it was a rugby club do.

Anyway, it was only when we turned up that we realised it was fancy dress – no-one had thought to tell us. Andy was wearing his full Ted outfit – drape jacket, winkle-picker shoes, boot lace tie and so on.

He got pretty fed up as people kept nudging him, saying "nice costume, mate," replying with increasing frustration "It's not fancy dress – I often wear this."

What really put the tin lid on it was when, near the end of the night, it was announced that he'd come third in the fancy dress contest. He wasn't amused – but took it well.

Andy was in the Home Guard darts team and the amount of drink he'd consumed was a crucial factor in his performance chucking the arrows. Stone cold sober he was rubbish, quite merry he was on fire, too much booze and his game went to pot again.

Yes, they were great times, those alcohol-fuelled days and nights with our old gang.

But to get back to yesterday, having sent my friend request and taken a bit of a trip down Memory Lane, I headed for the Bell (Seabourne's) , where I met and chatted to John Gaynor, John Palmer, Kelly Adams, Lee Robertson, Billy Clarkson and Tim Robbins.

It was a nice evening in my local pub with mates – just like I used to have before it changed hands five years ago and went downhill. Newest managers Mark and Laura, who took over last Christmas, are doing a grand job of restoring it to its former glory.

But, as usual these days, after a couple of pints I was ready to head home – and arriving back, I sat down just in time to watch an excellent programme on BBC Four.

A star-studded cast took part in an hour-long rendition of Dylan Thomas's brilliant Under Milk Wood. Sir Tom Jones, Michael Sheen, Charlotte Church, Katherine Jenkins, Griff Rhys Jones, Jonathan Pryce, Sian Phillips, Bryn Terfel, Tom Ellis and Robert Pugh were among those involved.

I've always loved this "play for voices" ever since studying it for O-level at school. It's a work of genius – the lyrical and poetic use of words is the best I've ever encountered. And I've read Shakespeare and most of the other great writers.

If you're not familiar with it, this spellbinding literary gem tells of a day in the lives of a group of colourful characters residing in a fictional Welsh seaside village.

The poetry is dazzling, beautiful and evocative but in places its tone is dark and earthy. Sex and death are prominent themes.

Even the village's name – Llareggub – is bugger all spelled backwards. It's widely thought to be based on Laugharne, a small fishing community in Carmarthenshire.

I thoroughly enjoyed once again hearing the vocalisation of this magical, wonderful classic.

No wonder Dylan Thomas is revered by poets and lyricists the world over. Under Milk Wood is a tour de force of imaginative and mesmerising wordplay.

The writer was born in Swansea in October 1914 – so this is his centenary year. But he was a heavy drinker and it seriously affected his health. He died in New York in November 1953, aged just 39. But his magnificent skill will live forever.

**June 3** – Time for two news updates. Firstly, we've been told that the search continues for Leicester girl Madeline McCann, who went missing during a family holiday in Portugal in 2007 when she was just three years old.

Metropolitan Police officers with sniffer dogs are helping their Portuguese colleagues explore a cordoned-off area of scrubland as they investigate Maddie's disappearance. It's a five-minute walk from the apartment where her family was staying.

The second update regards ongoing inquiries into child abuse allegations levelled against former TV star and charity champion Jimmy Savile. The claims now astonishingly number 500.

How many of them are actually true we will never know as he's had the audacity to die so they can no longer be tested in a law court – and I abide by the golden rule of justice that someone's innocent until proven guilty.

I wonder how many claimants are opportunistic band wagon jumpers – and why individuals waited many years to accuse him.

Of course, some might have been frightened, ashamed, confused or not sure they'd be believed. But all we have at this late stage are conjecture and possibilities.

Many people will feel that the pure volume of the allegations strongly suggests there's no smoke without fire. They will also point to the charging and prosecution of other (still living) top celebrities as a result of the ongoing investigation.

Our sex-crazed, wildly obsessive media has been a key player in this whole sordid issue with its reckless attempts to disgrace as many folk as possible, proudly parade its exclusives (whether true or not) and sell newspapers or retain viewers' attention.

But if even a fraction of the claims are true, I'd suspect a widespread cover-up attempt involving those in high places turning a blind eye while shielding the offenders from capture and punishment – until now. And that really would be a scandal – a disgrace.

**June 4** – Police have been digging into the earth on hilly wasteland at Praia da Luz on Portugal's Algarve in their continuing search for missing Maddie McCann.

Meanwhile, on home soil, we're about to have the last Queen's Speech before next May's general election.

This is when the monarch announces the government's plans for its new term in office – in this coalition's case, its last term.

Fracking, zero hours contracts, pension reforms and plastic bags are among the topics covered by 11 new bills due to be introduced during the next 11 months. All are highly controversial issues.

I've already told of my own opposition to fracking, zero hours contracts and the bid to bring in a 5p charge for plastic shopping bags.

The latter, I feel, has bog-all to do with protecting the environment and everything to do with charging us more while tightening control over our every movement.

Apart from detesting the whole idea of people having to pay for these flimsy, notoriously unreliable carriers, I think such a policy could possibly achieve the exact opposite of its stated intention.

It would either make little difference, or actually increase the use of bags that fall to bits before you get home - preventing their re-use, a form of recycling.

Why? – Because many people would go shopping, buy several at a time along with their other goods, (whether they need that many or not) and then stockpile them at home, using them liberally and creating more waste.

The really skint would struggle to afford this, of course – but there could well be millions who'd grumble for a while but still do it.

So it's hardly a Green initiative!  - And those who believe it is clearly haven't thought it through.

The old fashioned idea of going shopping with your own sturdy big bag or two – a great idea at the time – is dead and buried in our 21ˢᵗ-century use-and-chuck society, just like sock darning and shoe heeling.

I'm not saying this is right – it's just the way things are.

And a thought occurred to me the other day on checking the postal delivery at our big house converted to flats.

If the government was really serious about cutting waste and protecting our environment, surely it would have outlawed junk mail by now?

Thousands of trees a year could be saved and as many tons of waste prevented just by stopping every Tom, Dick and Harry shoving unsolicited paper adverts and appeals though our letterboxes.

Now that really would be a Green initiative making a proper difference!

**June 5** – Oh bum! - I've just received a letter telling me my publishers have gone bust. Makes me wonder what's going to happen to the six volumes of my life story already published and the seventh which was being printed up, due for publication soon. I guess I'll have to find out.

Meanwhile, I'm going to continue writing this eighth book in the Sunshine and Ice series while looking out for alternative publishers to continue putting my journal and lyrics out in the public domain – hopefully nice and cheaply!

It is a bit worrying, though, to think that my dream might prove to be short-lived and I could lose out on royalties. Hey ho.

But I've got so used to writing my life journal there's no question of me giving up until ill health forces me to.  If nothing else, it keeps me busy and is great therapy.

**June 6** – It was 70 years ago today that the Allied Forces staged the D-Day landings at Normandy, France.

World leaders and VIPs including Royalty have joined hundreds of medal-wearing veterans of on those famous beaches and also at Portsmouth – a major launching pad for the operation - to mark the occasion.

Thousands have turned up to honour them, millions of others been watching the church services and other commemorative events on TV.

For anyone who doesn't know, D-Day was a turning point in history and featured the largest seaborne invasion of all time.

A massive armada sailed to claim back German-occupied Western Europe. It led to the restoration of the French Republic and was a major factor in the Allies' victory in the Second World War.

We remember with sadness, thanks and great admiration the brave souls who gave their lives in a bid to save us from Hitler's evil Nazi regime.  And we respect and honour the survivors involved in this highly emotional commemoration.

Stuff the political animals and violent nut jobs that get us into these blood-drenched conflicts.  Sod the glory seekers and demented idiots spouting jingoistic poison.

It's the ordinary folk on the front lines I feel for - the ones with deeply moving tales of courage and camaraderie.

Behind all the pomp and ceremony, religion and rhetoric lay their stark stories of splintered bones and broken hearts, ripped flesh and tattered dreams.

Old soldiers who take part in these conflicts don't revel in nostalgic nationalism. They recall fallen comrades with tears in their eyes while yearning for the day that no-one has to make the ultimate sacrifice in battle ever again.

We should listen to them – they've been there, they know the grim reality of war.

Unlike the politicians who continue to embroil service personnel in their lethal ideological clashes while keeping themselves safe and sound in the comfort of their plush White House and Westminster offices. Despicable reptiles!

Turning from poignant history to modern times, there's a trendy phrase being used quite widely these days about people living life to the max.

Many folk, including most of my friends, associate the term with taking risks, pushing our bodies and nerves to the limit and getting as many thrills and as much excitement as possible. Sky diving, mountaineering, jetting off to exotic locations and suchlike.

I take a totally different view. Enjoying life to the max, living in the moment and not wasting a single second all mean something else entirely to me.

My largely quiet existence might seem relatively dull and boring to some. But I see it like this – I can thoroughly relish even the most mediocre and mundane moments if they're pleasant ones.

Let's face it, there's enough tragedy, pain and heartache about –
ask one of those D-Day veterans or someone who's just lost a
loved one in a car smash.

I say enjoy as many moments as you possibly can – even the
humdrum ones – because you never know when it's all going to
end.  That's the way I try to live my own life now, in between
the inevitable bouts of sadness and hassle.

I won't be jumping out of any planes or climbing any
mountains.  But I've already has some great times and aim to
carry on doing so, in my own calm and restrained way, while
I'm still able to.

Am I missing out? Many would say yes.  But that would be
them talking, not me. I'm quite happy as I am, thank you.

**June 9, evening** – Facebook has been going berserk this
afternoon as news spread of the shock death of comedy actor
Rik Mayall, aged just 56. The cause has not yet been revealed
of his demise at his London home – but police say it was not
suspicious.

One of his most famous roles was as pseudo-rebellious student
Rick in the groundbreaking television classic The Young Ones,
appearing alongside Adrian Edmondson, Nigel Planer,
Christopher Ryan and Alexei Sayle.

Also on TV, he was sleazy Tory MP Alan B'Stard in The New
Statesman, Lord Flashheart in Blackadder and Richie in
Bottom, where he co-starred with his great mate and long-
running comedy partner Ade Edmondson.

And he was part of the Comic Strip Presents team with Edmondson, Planer, Sayle, Peter Richardson, Jennifer Saunders, Dawn French, Robbie Coltrane and Keith Allen.

I was among millions of avid fans of this skilled and funny star who will be greatly missed.

**June 10** – There come certain times in our lives when we need to make hard decisions for the sake of our own welfare and peace of mind.

Properly supportive family members and true friends will understand, appreciate and respect our choices at these crucial junctures.  If anyone can't, that's their problem, not ours.

I think I might be at one of those stages now. Watch this space.

**June 11** – I'm currently half-way through reading Pete Townsend's autobiography Who I Am.  Well, more like two-thirds of the way through if we're going to get all accurate and pedantic about it.

I'd say this book is a must for all rock music fans. Published by Harper Collins, it's written in a highly-readable style with disarming honesty by a man who's been there and done it all with some of the most famous people on the planet.

Jagger, Clapton, Elton, Bowie, the Beatles, Hendrix – they're all here along with Townsend's Who colleagues Roger Daltrey, John Entwistle and Keith Moon plus a host of other rock icons. The stories are numerous, informative and very entertaining.

It's an absorbing study of the triumphs, turmoil and tragedy surrounding a guy who became a spokesman for a questioning, angry and rebellious generation.  It tells of the drink, the drugs, spiritual awakening, euphoria, lunacy and sad premature deaths.

I've always loved Townsend and the Who – I was part of that generation.

And for me, at their very best they trumped even the Rolling Stones.  I saw them at Poole in the early 1980s with Kenney Jones on drums following the dreadful demise of the legendary Keith Moon. And they were brilliant.

**June 12** – The World Cup kicks off in Brazil today with the opening ceremony followed by the host nation's match against Croatia.

England's first game is a tough one against four-times tournament winners Italy on Saturday.  With a four to five hour time difference, it's being shown live on our TVs here late evening.

Uruguay, cup winners twice in the early decades of the competition, are also in our group.  We've won the trophy once of course, beating West Germany 4-2 in the Wembley final in 1966 when the global event was staged on home soil.

It will be a joy to see the dazzling skills of the world's top footballers as they proudly sport their national teams' shirts and play for their countries – especially as so many of them are familiar faces from our own Premier League.

A party atmosphere is guaranteed in Brazil, a country known for its sunny climate, dancing, music and, of course, football – it's won the World Cup five times, more than any other nation.

But there's a jet black flipside to the land of samba, soccer and suntans – it's also reputed to be a place where human rights violations are rife.

It's supposedly a democracy, and yet slavery, forced labour, police brutality, summary executions and violence against children, women and certain ethnic groups are commonplace, say campaigning organisations like Amnesty International.

At the risk of sounding flippant, it seems to me like some people are far too keen to see such despicable attitudes and practices re-introduced here, albeit in a less extreme form (at least for now).

Maybe we should spare a thought for the victims of flagrant abuse in Brazil and other places as we enjoy the footballing fiesta while bathed in our own summer sunshine. Come on England!

Of course, the World Cup has been all over this week's news. But so have other, much more serious issues.

A big row has erupted among government ministers over alleged Islamic radicalism in Birmingham schools. And in Essex, a teacher apparently told a 10-year-old boy to remove a Help for Heroes charity wristband, saying it might offend Muslims.

Apart from thinking both these stories are part of a continuing spiteful campaign to cause friction between ethnic groups in our fair land, I must say that, if true, the extremism in schools claim shows a worrying trend.

I detest the whole idea of a dogmatic and intolerant religious or political emphasis being expressed through classroom curricula

- and let's not forget that English history is jam-packed with examples of this dating back over the centuries.

Okay, the faith in question was Christianity in its different forms, but the principle's exactly the same.  Schools should give children a taste of all religious and political ideas then leave it up to them to decide which they prefer – while respecting the right of others to make different choices.

And yes, paganism and atheism should be included in a fair and balanced summary of all the spiritual options.  The same golden rules should apply to political studies.

I guess what I'm saying is I hate indoctrination full stop. The English education system was riddled with it for hundreds of years.

I'd hoped we'd got more enlightened and tolerant since the 1960s - but the claims of a new kind of radicalism infesting Birmingham classrooms, centred on an alternative religious and political viewpoint, suggests not.  And this concerns me deeply.

Bigotry is deplorable, whether the targets are of a different culture, religion or race. Polish, Romanian and other Eastern European groups in our country seem to be as hated and reviled as Muslims.  It used to be blacks and Jews – still is in some places.

It's a narrow-minded, ignorant mindset that makes no sense to my spiritual viewpoint. Disliking certain types of people is an understandable, natural human response, but hating them based purely on their race or religion is just plain nuts.

Sure, being in a waiting room, a house, on a bus or in any other confined space with a bunch of people jabbering on in their own language can be quite intimidating if you're in a minority of one.

But just imagine how they feel when the boot's on the other foot - probably a lot more often. Okay, they're in our country and should expect it, blah blah blah. What I'm saying is a bit of two-way tolerance and respect can work wonders.

That's why the reports of a new form of rigid religious indoctrination in schools are shocking and very worrying.

It's also why I was pleased to see a pal's Facebook status yesterday, saying that those who moan about the Polish should bear in mind that a group of guys from that land provided our most successful fighter pilot squadron during the Battle of Britain.

My ex-squaddie pal's comment was "bloody Poles coming over here protecting our women and children!"

Witty and though-provoking – nice one, mate!

Turning to the boy's Help for Heroes wristband, I can't for the life of me see how on Earth this would upset Muslims anyway.

It shows that the wearer – or in the boy's case, probably his family - has donated to a charity helping maimed and wounded ex-service folk. That's all.

It certainly doesn't signify any support for the political decision to send combatants into battle. Neither does it suggest a dislike of Muslims or the backing of any kind of action harming them.

People of all political and religious persuasions have been killed and maimed in blood soaked conflicts over the years.

Muslims died in the 911 and London Bombs atrocities and no doubt in the two World Wars, the Falklands and Gulf campaigns.

Survivors of battles and terrorist attacks and the loved ones of those killed in them need help – and when governments fail to do this, charities feel compelled to step in.

Organisations like Help for Heroes provide practical assistance to the casualties of insane military clashes. Their efforts have nothing to do with politics, race or religion.

I think the wristband furore is yet another case of people getting faiths, racial issues and ideologies all badly mixed up in a warped, crazy mindset defying logic or reason.

Okay, before anyone else says it, I know the boy in question was said to be wearing the band in honour of Lee Rigby.

I'm also well aware that Army drummer Rigby was apparently dressed in a Help for Heroes tee-shirt when savagely butchered to death by two Islamic fundamentalists on a London street in broad daylight just over a year ago.

His killers said they were striking a blow for all Muslims murdered by the brutal Western imperialism that the fusilier represented.

The fact that he was wearing that tee shirt at the time means that his name – therefore the British Army and the hawkish politicians controlling it - will always be closely associated with the charity, for some in a very negative way.

Apparently, public donations rocketed after his murder shocked the nation. There was also a sharp rise in hostility towards Muslims.

But the way I see it, Rigby, a musician and family man, was just another of the victims from all sides sacrificed on the altar of ideological and political madness.  Ordinary, decent folk caught up in their crazy leaders' bold military ambitions.

I feel for the loved ones of every fallen combatant, regardless of cultural background. I say it's high time we drew a line in the sand and called a halt to this seemingly endless struggle during which all suffer and no-one ultimately wins.

It's a crying shame our political overlords don't appear to share my view.

A couple of months ago, we had Cameron and Blair's clumsy, insensitive and inflammatory comments, mentioned in chapter two.

Now we've got US president Barack Obama saying his government is considering military action among options to help Iraq fight Islamic militants in its own civil war.

Syria continues to be torn apart by sectarian violence as English Muslims become radicalised against what they see as imperialist Western aggression.

And so it goes on – and on, and on.  Ye gods!

**June 13** – Europe met South America in last night's opening match of the World Cup as Croatia played Brazil.  The hosts won 3-1.  We footie fans look forward to a great tournament, with England winning the final.  Well, we can dream!

Turning from sport to other news, it seems Rik Mayall died from heart failure.  His wife, Barbara Robbins, is reported to have said he "suffered an acute cardiac event" at their home after returning from a morning run on Monday. He died soon afterwards.

Her comments follow the West London Coroner's Office saying the post-mortem examination had proved inconclusive and further tests were required.

Another lyric has been forming itself in my addled brain. It's about Glastonbury and its music festival.  And it's a bit of a tribute to William Blake's Jerusalem.  Here it is:


***Soul Connections***

                      ***Martin Money, June 12-13, 2014.***


*Sacred feet in times gone by once graced these verdant hills*
*Now they're known for tents and vans and music, pills and thrills*
*Cash and trinkets, booze and fast food, fairground rides and screams*
*Joyful faces daubed with glitter, multi-coloured dreams*

*Grass and dancing, mud and laughter, celebrating life*
*Seeking answers, freeing minds, eschewing humdrum strife*
*Truth and wisdom, peace and healing, hope for better days*
*Looking to a brighter future, searching for the ways*

*Soak them up, those sounds and sights*
*Let the beats and dazzling lights*
*Wake your spirit from its slumber*
*You're a star - not just a number, star not just a number*

*Ancient legends fill the air at England's holy heart*
*Seeping from the trees and land, old rhythms and new art*
*Loving vibes and soul connections, one community*
*Modern means to find the past – our precious Glastonbury.*

**June 14** – Day two of the World Cup provided its first shocking result with defending champions Spain going down 5-1 to a rampant Holland. One of the best defences in the world looked flat-footed and ordinary as the Dutch ripped them apart with breath-taking agility and speed.

It was like the mesmerising Holland of old – before they got far too brutal and dirty during the last World Cup, when Spain beat them in the final.

Tonight it's England against Italy. Come on Roy's boys!

**June 14 – five hours later** – Man, I'm buzzing! Why? – Because I've just had a visit from Phil, Emily, Chloe and Lucas (Harvey was with Em's mum). As it's Father's Day tomorrow, they brought along two cards - one from the couple and the other from the children – plus a five-CD box set called Rock Anthems as my present. Nice one guys – really sweet!

**June 15** – All in all, yesterday, a Saturday, was a good 'un. After the fab family visit, I got a text from my mate Sam inviting me to her and Carl's later in the day where they staged a barbeque in the sunshine.

Sam's cousin Jac came over from New Milton – a few train stops along the line – and others present were Sam's son Alex, his girlfriend Charley, our mutual pal Tina Mcauley, Sam and Carl's two little boys Rudy and Bailey, family pet dogs Albert and Blaze, and – briefly - our friend Sharon Pendleton.

Sam's daughter Bec joined us later when she finished work in an ice cream and fast food kiosk on the Southbourne cliff top. Russell Hall, Alex and Bec's dad, also turned up later and so did a guy called Jimmy.

As usual, Carl was in the charge of cooking the food – a role he seems more than happy to take.

Getting home, I sat down to watch the England versus Italy World Cup match on telly. Our lads played really well – good, confident, attractive attacking football – but were beaten 2-1.

Losing their opening game so narrowly to a fine team like Italy was no disgrace at all, especially considering how impressively they performed.  Now they have to beat Uruguay on Thursday and Costa Rica next Tuesday to proceed to the knock-out stage.

They can do it – of course they can.  They just have to think positive, keep on playing like they did and ignore the irritating doom and gloom merchants sharpening their knives while saying it's already all over.  Negative nitwits!

I'm playing one of my Father's day rock compilation CDs as I write this and Phil sent me a really nice Facebook message earlier.

**June 16** – Following on from the Birmingham schools controversy, we now have news of an even more alarming turn of events.

It's said that young English Muslim men, radicalised by hard-liners in this country, are going out in their hundreds to fight alongside like-minded Islamic militants in Iraq and Syria's civil wars.

David Cameron's response to these allegations has been uncharacteristically feeble –merely blathering on about tolerance and democracy.

What he should be doing, of course, is ordering an immediate in-depth inquiry to find out if there's any truth in the claims.

And if so, to investigate why these young men became so disenchanted, bitter and ultimately violent.

Because until such vital questions are asked and answered, the situation's just going to get progressively worse.

If I can see this, why the flipping 'eck can't he?  Maybe he's choosing not to, for to launch such a probe might really set the cat among the pigeons.

How so? – By unearthing certain ugly, disturbing, and - for him and other political leaders - seriously awkward, inconvenient and pretty damning facts about their own attitudes and behaviour in dealing with ethnic issues and foreign affairs.

Our PM's seemingly timid refusal to act looks so incongruous in light of his usual tendency to poke his nose in uninvited, meddling in issues that shouldn't concern him.

Tony Blair's apparently already come out saying Iraq's bloody sectarian war isn't a result of the US/UK invasion ordered by him and George W Bush in the wake of 911.

Methinks the lady doth protest too much! Why on Earth should he feel the need to say this? – Guilty conscience? (Especially bearing in mind there was very scant evidence that Iraq took any part in that particular terrorist attack).

Interestingly, even a correspondent for the dear old conservative BBC said this morning that, although he was a brutal dictator, Saddam Hussein at least held his country together and since his deposition, it had become seriously unstable.

Did no-one tell these clowns you can't invade a territory, traumatise its people and then just walk away? Actions have consequences guys!

Meanwhile, talks are going on with neighbouring Iran to see if anything can be done to neutralise the extremists and ease the tension.

You know, Iran, the nation once ruled by the Ayatollah Khomeini, public enemy number one during the Iran-Iraq War, when we helped arm Hussein to fight him.

Dirty business politics, innit?

**June 17** – Obama has announced the sending of 275 armed troops to Iraq "to protect the American embassy." He's warned more might follow if the situation worsens.

An Islamic group called Isis, apparently comprising violet extremists, is said to have led an uprising that's ripping the country to pieces.

So who are Isis? Well, we're told they're a militant outfit intent on enforcing a radical Islamic state in that troubled land.

The Independent newspaper states: "With its multi-pronged assault across central and northern Iraq in the past one and a half weeks, the Islamic State of Iraq and the Levant (Isis) has taken over from the al-Qaida organisation founded by Osama bin Laden as the most powerful and effective extreme jihad group in the world."

So now we know. Or do we? Depends which side of the ideological divide you find yourself standing, I guess. Those English Muslims going off to fight in the Middle East have obviously got so fed up with the way things are done here that they've decided a hard line Islamic system's a better option.

But we have to be so very careful when bandying about emotive terms like "hard line", "militant", "extremist", "terrorist", "radical" and "fundamentalist."

In some Muslims' eyes, the West, led by the United States and Europe, is all of these and Isis is made of brave and devout believers in pure Islamic doctrines, determined to defend, promote and spread them in order to make the world a better place.

For my part, I simply despise with a passion any hate-fuelled, belligerent, violent extremism - regardless of which side it arises from in any ideological battle.

I've said it before, more than once, and I'll continue doing so until I draw my last breath – one man's terrorist is another man's freedom fighter, and which is which very much depends on the culture and beliefs you support.

I am not, in any way, shape or form, an apologist for warmongering organisations wreaking death and destruction. They're all as bad as each other – including those sanctioned by so-called democratically elected governments.

I'm a man of peace – a pacifist. Violence repels me.

But we have to remember why we have such distinctions, divisions and blood-stained clashes.  It's because those in power want it that way.  They cold-heartedly set groups up against each other – racial, religious, political, doesn't matter to them – in order to cause resentment, create friction, split communities and thereby keep control.

Yes, we keep coming back to it, time and time again. Good old divide and rule.

Speaking of which, there was a disturbing documentary on Channel Five TV last night called Benefits Britain: Life on the Dole.

Set in Great Yarmouth, it was as grim, depressing and thought-provoking as Channel Four's recent series called Benefits Street, centred on a Birmingham housing estate.

Yes, this is the dark underbelly of England that government ministers blithely choose to ignore.  As they prattle on ridiculously and outrageously about economic recovery, this is how many citizens in our beleaguered nation are forced to live.

Here's the stark, unpalatable reality, no matter how ferociously the callous and crazy politicians try to dress it up as their success story.

It's a regrettable, seemingly endless saga of ordinary people caught in a vicious spiral of money troubles and constant worry - the unfortunate victims of financial fascism.

Watching the programme, I thought how easily it could have been about my town - Bournemouth.

Great Yarmouth is a similar seaside resort where most of the jobs are already taken and the only vacancies arising are seasonal ones totally reliant on the tourist trade.

And, just like Bournemouth, it's a multi-cultural community. Some of the benefit claimants interviewed were angry and hostile towards people from other national backgrounds who ran and staffed local shops or ignored minimum wage regulations to offer or take cash-in-hand jobs paying £2 less an hour than the legal limit.

I understand their frustration - and their belief that long-term residents are at the back of the queue when it comes to gaining employment and escaping the benefits system.

The same applies to housing and other facilities in many people's eyes.

No wonder Nigel Farage and his UKIP party proved so popular at the recent European and local council elections. This deeply unsatisfactory state of affairs clearly prevails across the country.

The documentary glaringly showed just how miserably Tory, Labour and now coalition governments have all failed to address growing problems, displaying unbelievable incompetence while employing disastrously lax immigration rules.

Now, using the old divide and rule tactic, they disgracefully set up immigrants and benefits claimants as their whipping boys to take the rap – amazingly axing and savagely cutting back already paltry welfare payments. Despicable gits!

Claimants aren't on benefits for fun. They'd love to join the rest of society and have more cash and better lifestyles.  But the jobs simply aren't there – or of they are, they're illegally low-paid ones snapped up by immigrants far too willing to take them.

Getting all authoritarian about it and withdrawing people's benefits just causes more misery while doing absolutely nothing to help.  Ensuring more real job vacancies are made available would be a far better way of starting to solve the problems.

But for Cameron and crew to outrageously claim that this is exactly what they're doing when the evidence suggests the complete opposite really takes the biscuit.

One young guy in the TV programme had settled into a routine of working at the local holiday camp in summer and going back on the dole for the winter when they didn't need him.  And he was among the lucky ones.

The sooner uncaring, out-of-touch politicians start recognising and addressing such pressing issues properly – helping relieve hardship instead of unfairly punishing easy targets – the better, I'd say.

But they're not going to, are they?  They're the master manipulators, kings of divide and rule, and it suits them just fine that the angry and bitter are blaming other groupings – notably foreigners - and not them.

It would serve them bloody well right if Farage and UKIP swept to power in next year's general election.  But that's a prospect that chills my bones, for I fear such a backlash could have even more disastrous consequences for our country.

But before we start thinking its all doom and gloom, we're hopelessly screwed so we might as well reach for the razor blades, here's a little ray of hope.

Motor racing legend Michael Schumacher is finally out of his coma, out of hospital and on the road to recovery.  He was admitted in a critical condition with a serious head injury after a fall while skiing six months ago.

No doubt there are loads of other good and heart-warming things happening across the globe.  It's just a great shame that the media seems so obsessed with the bad stuff.

**June 18** – My dear Mum passed over 17 years ago today. I've lit a candle for her and put a little tribute on Facebook.  Even now there's not a day goes by I don't think of her and Dad. The deep hurt remains and even though the scars heal over with time, the wounds lie just below the surface – forever.

I can't help wondering where the heck those 17 years went – gone in the blink of an eye, it seems.  The older you get, the faster time whizzes by.  Forget clocks and calendars – this is the indisputable truth.

There was more on the news this morning about the global ideological war, with a bold assertion that there are more jihadis (Islamic militants) in Britain than anywhere else in Europe.

The fear is that radicalised British Muslims signing up to fight in Syria and Iraq could return hardened by warfare, skilled in guerrilla tactics and bomb making, and ready to wreak havoc.

But, bearing in mind what I said two days ago, isn't this frankly terrifying warning a little bit like shutting the stable door after the horse has bolted?

If the claim, highlighted in the Daily Mail (yes, I know!) is true, by the time these young men come back it will be far too late to stop their murderous ambitions in their tracks. Our only hope then would be to catch them before they did any damage.

The real answer, as I've already suggested, would be to find out as a matter of urgency why such people become so embittered and militant in the first place.

We need to nip such problems and friction in the bud – not wait until minds have been poisoned by violent notions. But, of course, that would be against the whole ethos of divide and rule thinking, which is probably why it's not being seriously considered.

**June 19** – There was an excellent TV documentary about history a few years ago in which the narrator, former Monty Python star Terry Jones, said our nation had taught others all they know about so-called holy wars, terrorism and ethnic cleansing, pointing out that we had been guilty of all three for centuries.

I've already made the point that hard line indoctrination in English schools is far from new and it's just the religion in question that seems to have changed.

Not only did parents have little or no choice in what faith – or even version of it - their children were taught by compulsion, the brutal enforcement and bloodstained history of that belief system came with some pretty powerful military imagery.

Warrior themes about fighting the good fight are rife. A famous hymn is actually entitled Onward Christian Soldiers and there's even an organisation called the Salvation Army in which both men and women dress in mock military uniforms and distribute a magazine named the War Cry.

Of course the vast majority of believers from all sections of the faith are peace-loving folk who wouldn't dream of actually blowing up buildings or waging real warfare. But some unhinged nutters, swayed by the emotive imagery and confrontational rhetoric, could do. The same is no doubt true in other religions.

And, thinking about it, a Salvationist in uniform wearing a Remembrance poppy might – just might - have the same unsettling effect on someone with a different belief as a real British soldier sporting a Help for Heroes tee-shirt.

A lot less muscular aggression and a lot more peaceful tolerance all round are called for when dealing with spiritual matters as well as racial and cultural ones, I'd suggest.

*****************************************

# CHAPTER FIVE – DANCING IN THE RAIN

**June 20** – Oh dear! England lost to Uruguay yesterday so their World Cup dream is almost over. Liverpool's Luis Suárez scored twice as the South Americans beat Roy's boys 2-1.

On paper, even losing their first two matches in a World Cup tournament for the first time ever doesn't automatically mean elimination, because of the way results have gone elsewhere in the group.

But Italy must beat Costa Rica later today for England to stand any chance at all. Gerrard and co would then have to defeat Costa Rica by a wide margin next Tuesday and hope and pray that Italy trounce Uruguay. That way we could scrape through on goal difference.

Any other results and our lads are on the plane home. But there was one bit of good news in their sorry saga so far – Their one goal yesterday was scored by Wayne Rooney, breaking his World Cup tournament duck.

Let's hope he and his team can find the net plenty of times on Tuesday while all the other results from this point on go in their favour.

Defending champions Spain are out. They lost their first two matches and other teams' score lines have ensured that, even if they win their last group game against Australia on Monday, they're still not going through to the knock-out stage.

Switching from football to music, I'm pleased to report that I bought Paloma Faith's album on CD a few days ago and it's very good. The songs are strong, the band good and tight and Paloma has a terrific voice. This is modern soul at its best.

I bought the album on a friend's recommendation and I'm certainly not disappointed.

Speaking of friends, my good mate Sam Excell recently had a new tattoo drawn on her lower leg. It's a saying: "Life's not about waiting for the storm to pass; it's about learning to dance in the rain."

Like her, I thought this a great piece of advice so I decided to find out where it came from and who first said it.

It seems to be the handiwork of one Vivian Greene - visionary, artist, author and entrepreneur, whose stated aim is to spread a message of greater love and awareness to everyone on the planet.

Vivian also enables artists, authors, photographers, speakers and fellow visionaries to serve others and prosper by turning their works into inspirational products.

Now THERE'S someone who truly promotes the positive vibe. Good on her – we desperately need such wise and compassionate souls to bring a bit of joy to a world of pain, misery and dark negativity.

Another of her sayings is: "All that is real is seen with the heart." Terrific!

A similarly very inspirational person was Stephen Sutton, the teenager who raised millions of pounds for cancer sufferers with his upbeat, warm and witty internet postings bravely defying his own sad plight - dying from the illness.

Someone said on the day of his funeral that Steve chose to light a candle rather than curse the darkness.  Again, I thought this was a brilliant way of encapsulating the positive spin some folk put on things even in the face of apparent hopelessness.

It seems the speaker was paraphrasing an old Chinese proverb. What an excellent one it is!

I've got the TV on in the background as I type this and the Jeremy Kyle Show has just started.  It's the usual parade of moronic, ignorant, aggressive, shouty blokes and birds – and that's just the audience!

**June 21** – It's the summer solstice, the year's longest day and my mother's birthday. I've lit another candle for her – RIP Mum.

Costa Rica beat Italy 1-0 yesterday – so England are out, even if they score loads on Tuesday. Rats!

Mind you, if they do, it will boost their confidence no end and, as a mate of mine said, this new team is still a work in progress.

Okay, the defence needs tightening up and they all have to learn to communicate better, but they played some good attacking football against Italy although they lost.

Give manager Roy Hodgson a bit more time and the promising young players more international experience and we could have a good side ready for the 2016 Euros.

Am I deluded optimist? Maybe, but isn't that what being an England fan's all about these days? I hate the way some people are so negative, easily discouraged and far too quick to slate and abandon their national team the moment things go pear-shaped.

Keep the faith guys – keep the faith!

Switching from sport to politics, I see "Red Ed" Miliband has turned a rather ugly shade of blue.

He apparently said yesterday that unemployed youngsters should be forced to attend training schemes in order to continue receiving benefits.

This seems very heavy-handed, un-socialist and, frankly, pretty damned Tory to me.

Sure, training schemes should be in place for those who feel they need to gain basic or specialist skills. It would equip them better for any jobs that might become available.

But surely this should be a voluntary thing, not compulsory? Many wouldn't need to go on such courses. To force them to seems unduly draconian, punitive and a waste of money, time and energy.

The money would be far more effectively spent in real job creation and the time and energy much better used helping jobless folk who are able and eager to work to seek out and apply for any suitable vacancies on offer.

What's the point in training people and making them ready for employment when it's just not there for them?       The government should also be seriously providing new, proper opportunities for paid work – or at least enabling employers to.

But Miliband's comment suggests that if he and his Labour pals win the next election they're just going to carry on in the same vein as the coalition – penalising benefit claimants while doing nothing to provide the work that would get them off welfare.

Meanwhile, David Cameron continues to bang on about an alleged over-spend on the benefits budget.   But what exactly does this mean?

An over-spend arises when you're running up a deficit or you don't want to pay out so much money on something. Your views and actions rely totally on your priorities.

Commercial businesses are based on profit and loss book-keeping.  Essential services ruddy well shouldn't be!

I notice dodgy David doesn't refer to an over-spend on tons of metal and other materials for a glossy multi-billion pound high speed rail link that we've managed without up to now.

Neither does he seem to mind paying out millions of pounds of our money to help people dying in poverty and squalor abroad.

Quite rightly too – we SHOULD be providing financial and practical help to our fellow human beings who desperately need it.  I'm not questioning this principle – I firmly support it – its Cameron's screwed-up, inconsistent attitudes I'm opposing.

And especially his savage reluctance to look after and pay money helping people down on their luck in his own country. That's what really appals and sickens me.

**June 22** – Happy birthday Stevie boy! Steve Yarwood, that is, my very good buddy of many years.

Young Steve (57 today) seems to have done another disappearing act of late, cutting himself off from everyone and keeping himself to himself again like he did before. I hope he's doing okay.

More sad news has hit the world of comedy – Patsy Byrne has died aged 80.  She played many roles on TV – funny and straight – but is probably best known as the kind but dim Nursie to Miranda Richardson's Queen Elizabeth 1st in Blackadder.

**June 23** – Two thoughts occurred to me earlier today as I sat on a wooden bench in the hot sunshine looking out over the sea at Southbourne cliff top.

The first, quite profound, was that this was one of life's truly exquisite moments – simple, free of charge but so very, very enjoyable.

Waves rippled and the water sparkled as it reflected the clear blue cloudless sky and bright sunlight. The outlook was clear and the view outstanding.

Yet this is the kind of thing we can so easily take for granted, especially if we're lucky enough to live so close to the coastline – in my case, a 15-minute walk.

My second thought was more mundane and concerned the scruffy appearance of the cliff top area itself that spoiled the beautiful vista if you looked either left or right.

The uncut grass was seriously overgrown and the litter bins hadn't been emptied so unsightly rubbish was spilling out on to the ground.

I wondered if the council was saving on maintenance costs or simply hadn't got round to tidying it up for the big tourist influx at the height of the summer season.

And I hoped it was the latter, for those thousands of visitors won't be too impressed if it's still like that.  It usually looks so neat, well-kept and attractive by now.

**June 24** – It's apparently midsummer's day, the sun's blazing down and it's absolutely sweltering.

Meanwhile, good old David Cameron continues to do sod all to take the heat out of the radicalised Muslims controversy.  But he is starting to say the right things - just starting, mind.

He was on the TV news yesterday evening stating that we as a nation should take decisive action to stop this process before it starts. Problem is he doesn't make any practical suggestions as to how we should do this.

In fact, he's only really stating the bleeding obvious.

Of course these young men should be dissuaded from taking hard line Islamic attitudes BEFORE they're converted to violent causes and go off to fight abroad - with the real possibility they could return to continue their so-called holy war here.

And diabolical Dave doesn't even attempt to ask that crucial question –why? What put these guys on a path possibly ending with their wreaking death and destruction?

Something must be seriously wrong here, in England (or Wales or Scotland) to enrage them so much and turn them so bitter. Until the root cause is recognised and dealt with, nothing will improve.

In fact, Cameron's newly belligerent stance on the issue yesterday will only further inflame the situation. Like I said, an urgent investigation is needed to identify and address the reasons for all the hatred and killing in a bid to prevent further bloodshed.

Speaking of which, the Queen was in Northern Ireland this morning. One of her stops was at the notorious Crumlin Road Jail.

Men, women and children were all held at the prison at various times from its opening in 1845 to its closure in 1996. Now it's a museum offering guided tours.

Inside, the Royal couple were met by a number of dignitaries, including Northern Ireland's First Minister Peter Robinson and Deputy First Minister Martin McGuinness.

The intriguing point is that both these men were detained at Crumlin Road a few decades ago at high points in the province's centuries-old, bloodstained civil war, quaintly called the Troubles.

So the Royal visit was highly symbolic of the progress made since 1998 when the Good Friday Agreement paved the way to peace after 400 years of fighting between Catholics and Protestants - or rather, violent political activists using the descriptions.

A few years ago such an event would have been unthinkable.

So here's another case of people being killed and maimed seemingly in the name of religion – in this instance, two diametrically opposed factions of the same faith.

Maybe if the root cause of all that friction, violence and death had been properly addressed right at the beginning, before the situation got seriously out of hand, those centuries of murder and misery might have been prevented.  Just saying.

**June 25** – England's last World Cup game was a goalless draw against Costa Rica. So they end up bottom of their group match table with just one point as they head for home.  But it's all good experience - so they say.

There have been positives.  At times they played well, especially against Italy, but these young stars need to get a lot more used to working together at this top level and improve both individually and jointly in the run-up to the Euros in two years' time.

If they can, they might do very well.  The present's a bit depressing but the future's looking good. Yep. I'm a typical England fan, eternally optimistic.

In the meantime it looks like the time's ripe to say a fond farewell to seasoned campaigners Steven Gerrard and Frank Lampard and thank them for all their outstanding work.  Both have done their country proud over the years.

Unlike Uruguayan striker Luis Suárez, who's seemingly been at it again.

Global football governing body FIFA has opened disciplinary proceedings against Suárez after he appeared to sink his teeth into the shoulder of Italy's Giorgio Chiellini during the two teams' last group game yesterday.

This is apparently the third time Suárez, who plays for Liverpool, has been caught biting opponents during matches. He could face a 24-match ban if found guilty.

Uruguay won 1-0 and go through to the knock-out phase. The result means that four-times tournament winners Italy are out.

With the score at 0-0, Suárez was seen to lean into Chiellini and apparently bite him on the shoulder.

He wasn't punished by the referee during the game but FIFA, intervening later, said the proceedings related to infringements that "might have escaped the match officials' attention."

Up to that point, the brilliant goal ace seemed to be finally shaking off his bad boy reputation following previous biting incidents. He was the English Premier League's top scorer last season and fast becoming one of this World Cup's major stars.

Seems to me something's not quite right in his head and he badly needs treatment to deal with his quick temper. He's his own worst enemy and his dirty tactics take the shine off his dazzling skills.

His behaviour sets a disgraceful example to millions of impressionable young fans.

And talking of disgraceful examples, I think that Suárez's antics and the apparent radicalisation of young Muslim men are both indicative of a far, far wider problem that seriously infests society and affects us all.

Egocentric parents with screwed-up priorities pass on deeply flawed ideas to their children. Clueless guardians let youngsters run wild with no concepts of boundaries, consideration of others, respect or self-discipline.

Even kind, loving adults unwittingly impart completely the wrong views and values; such is the totally twisted nature of the reality we all inhabit.

This alarming trend is reinforced by some very dubious messages picked up in classrooms and playgrounds and from the media - TV, internet, video games and suchlike.

Children and young people end up indoctrinated and brainwashed by life's worst aspects and start acting accordingly.

The positive vibration has real trouble breaking through all this negativity as kids grow into aggressive, violent, suspicious, bigoted, dishonest or self-centred adults.

We then see them on the TV news spouting hate-filled rants while clasping machine guns, or maybe ripping chunks out of each other physically or verbally on the Jeremy Kyle Show.

And so the spiral continues and intensifies. Bad attitudes aren't confined to Muslims or any other section of society. They're everywhere, eating through the very fabric of existence. That positive vibe is struggling but man do we need it – more than ever.

**June 26** – The allegations being levelled against the late Jimmy Savile seem to get more outrageous and shocking by the day.

Apart from the much-publicised child rape and abuse claims, we now have assertions that he also had sex with mental patients and corpses. Yes, dead people.

All were said to have happened in NHS hospitals, where staff were also said to have been indecently assaulted by the famous TV star.

The growing catalogue of stomach-turning accusations can never be tested in a law court as he's passed on. We will never know for sure the extent of his guilt or innocence. It just looks really, really bad.

Suggestions that young children, mental patients and the departed were involved might partly answer my earlier question as to why no-one reported the apparent misdemeanours at the times they were said to have occurred.

But I still suspect strong elements of sick glory-hunting, spiteful mischief-making and shameless bandwagon-jumping in this whole sorry, sordid saga.

Savile can't be punished now. But even if a fraction of the claims are true, some people MUST have known what was going on. It's inconceivable that they didn't.

In which case, there's been a massive cover-up operation lasting decades and those involved who are still alive should ruddy well be brought to book.

I have a horrible feeling that in fact these despicable people – some guilty of serious sexual and other crimes themselves – will simply close ranks and carry on offending.

And this will continue to happen, especially in the higher echelons of society, regardless of any truths or falsehoods in the Savile case.

He and other celebrities will be the ones accused, vilified and in some cases punished while their evil overlords and paymasters get off scot-free because they remain shielded and  protected by a very powerful but sick and twisted establishment.

I guess I take the same attitude towards sex crimes as I do converts to violence, all types of repulsive behaviour and any other of life's unwanted aspects.  And that is – recognise and deal with issues at source to neutralise them before any damage is done.

If we managed as a society to do this a lot more effectively, the positive results could be pretty frigging amazing.

**June 27** – It was exactly 30 years ago that my Dad boarded the train for the next station of existence. I've lit a candle for him and put a little tribute on Facebook. Blimey! - three decades gone - just where, exactly?

Not a day goes by without me missing his physical presence, humour, kindness and wisdom.  He was exactly 68 and a half years old when cancer claimed his body - but his spirit lives on through his descendants and he remains in my heart forever.

Well, FIFA has banned Luis Suárez from playing football, or even training, for four months.  Good – this sends out a clear message that such behaviour won't be tolerated.  It's a shame he wasn't also told to get counselling before coming back.

Still, his punishment for biting an Italian player on the shoulder means he'll take no further part in Uruguay's current World

Cup campaign.  He'll also miss Liverpool's first nine matches in the new Premier League season.  An appeal has been lodged.

Getting back briefly to the thorny subjects of welfare cuts and foreign workers, I feel I must clarify something I wrote earlier this month - to avoid any misunderstanding.

I commented that I understood and sympathised with the resentment felt by benefit claimants who saw their meagre payments reduced or stopped while relative newcomers to our shores grabbed the few work opportunities – legal or otherwise.

My phrase that may have caused confusion was a reference to politicians with "disastrously lax immigration rules."

It might well have appeared to contradict what I wrote in a previous book about my disgust at Enoch Powell and his supporters trying to stop people exercising their rights as British citizens to come over here from the old Commonwealth countries.

I still stand firmly by that - we gave such folk British passports after invading and colonising their territories in the days of the old British Empire, later re-named the Commonwealth.

It was therefore immoral to try and prevent them coming here, no matter what Powell said and others have continued to repeat. It's unfair, unjust and, quite frankly, racist.

But times have moved on and we've become more and more embroiled in the European Union with its high-handed orders for us to take large populations of immigrants, many from the continent's Eastern side – Poland, Romania and so on.

Instead of strongly resisting these ridiculously excessive demands, past Labour and Tory governments have both meekly complied without a whimper of protest. That's the far too lax immigration policies I was alluding to.

I have absolutely nothing against Eastern Europeans, any more than I have against any other nationalities. That would be bigoted, ignorant and belie my principles.

It's common sense really – racism doesn't enter into it. Commonwealth residents have a strong, historical claim to come and settle here; Eastern Europeans and others would have limited, negotiable and by no means automatic rights had our leaders not caved in to the EU.

Or at least they wouldn't be arriving here in the huge numbers this oppressive European super-state dictates.

And, like I've already said, compassion should also be carefully exercised whenever dealing with such emotive matters. There, I hope I've cleared up any misconceptions!

**June 28** – It's a Saturday – and that time of year again. Glasto's on telly in all its diverse glory.

Yesterday, we had John Newman, the Kaiser Chiefs, Lily Allen, Blondie, Haim, Paulo Nutini, Rudimental, Elbow and my favourite act so far, Arcade Fire.

Today, there's Robert Plant, Metallica, the Pixies, Jake Bugg, Goldfrapp, Bryan Ferry, Royal Blood and the Manic Street Preachers.

And tomorrow we have Dolly Parton, Kasabian, the Black Keys, Ed Sheeran, Massive Attack, Disclosure, the Black Eyed Peas and Ellie Goulding to look forward to.

Others appearing include Yoko Ono, London Grammar, the Wailers, Dr Feelgood, Clannad, Alison Moyet, Nick Lowe, Suzanne Vega, Billy Bragg and the Selecter.

There's something very special about Glastonbury that sets it apart from all the other festivals. Its legendary setting – at England's spiritual heart – and the wonderfully eclectic nature of the event makes it unique.

The spell cast by the event is so powerful you can pick it up through your TV set.

So many great acts over the years have been caught up in the vibe and the moment, inspired to lift their performances to new levels of excellence – adding a sublime extra dimension, if you like.

No doubt this year will be the same – and indeed it's already happened once with the brilliant, highly original Canadian band Arcade Fire raising their game while clearly loving the whole experience and saying it's the best gig they've ever played.

And speaking of Robert Plant, I'm pleased as punch to have secured tickets to see the former Led Zeppelin front man when he brings his new band to Boscombe's O2 Academy just along the road from here in November.  Excited? – well, just a bit!

What with going to see Gary Numan at the same venue in two days' time and heavy rockers Saxon there in December, it's already looking like being the second good year running for rock shows attended by yours truly. Cool!

**June 30, lunchtime** – Glastonbury was as good as ever and I thoroughly enjoyed catching some great performances on TV, some live, others recorded and shown later.

Personal highlights this year included Jake Bugg, Ellie Goulding, Blondie, Bryan Ferry, Dolly Parton, Lily Allen, Robert Plant, Disclosure, Ed Sheeran, the Kaiser Chiefs, Royal Blood, the Black Keys and the Manic Street Preachers.

Saturday headliners Metallica were mighty good but I still question whether this is the right festival for full on, loud and proud heavy metal - far better suited to Reading.

I especially loved Friday night bill-toppers Arcade Fire, who drew from so many different and varied influences to serve up a mesmerising mix of musical mastery.

And I'll be out and about in Boscombe this evening for another sonic treat – Gary Numan in concert. Looking forward to it and listening to an album of his right now to get me in the mood.

By the way, I'd like to wish a very happy birthday to my great mate Tom Jones. I sent him a text this morning.

**July 1** – Gary Numan was excellent. Like all the finest performers, he's impressive on record but far better in the flesh. All the hits were there, including a magnificent re-working of Are Friends Electric, which he did as an encore.

His band was terrific, too. All in all, another highly enjoyable rock show. It's the first time I've seen Numan in concert. I've always liked his music but in truth I've never been a massive fan, but last night he totally won me over.

Needless to say, I'd go see him again without hesitation if he played another local gig and I'd advise my friends to check him out too.

Well, that's my news. Now to turn to the national headlines. Rolf Harris has been convicted of 12 indecent assaults on four girls in the 1960s, 1970s and 1980s.

Come again?! Rolf Harris? Amiable, cuddly, funny, multi-talented Rolf, family favourite for over 50 years? No – you've got that wrong, surely? Really? REALLY? Flippin' 'eck!

Just goes to show how even the most likeable and apparently wholesome of TV stars are in reality flawed individuals - like us. They, too, have problems, issues and dark traits. Only the type and seriousness vary, therefore the scale of impact on others.

The big difference is that it seems so especially stunning when we're told something like this about a much-loved household name – an icon. But why? Why do we expect celebrities to be perfect when in all honesty none of us are?

Rolf Harris was a national treasure. Now it seems his glittering career will end in a prison cell. How long for, we'll know later this week when sentence is passed.

The 84-year-old Australian-born entertainer, now living in Bray, near Maidenhead, Berkshire, arrived in London in 1952, becoming a regular fixture on TV screens for decades as a children's entertainer, songwriter, artist and musician.

A holder of the MBE, OBE and CBE honorary medals, he rubbed shoulders with the upper echelons and even painted a portrait of the Queen to mark her 80th birthday.

Like most people of my age, I'm gob smacked and pretty ruddy unnerved to learn that a man we all adored and considered a very admirable good guy was apparently a really nasty piece of work on the quiet – an arrogant, ruthless sexual predator.

I saw him in summer season at Bournemouth once while on holiday here with my parents – and he was brilliant.

There were no signs of his sinister aspect, and even though I considered some of his X-rated jokes surprisingly blue for a so-called family entertainer, I didn't give it too much thought at the time.

But returning to the present day, I'm now thinking that perhaps I should explain myself quickly before people go off with the wrong impression.

When I say we all have our dark sides so we shouldn't expect too much of the famous, I fully accept that few of us are as bad as Rolf Harris is now portrayed.

I'm also very well aware of the social responsibility placed on celebrities in all fields to set good examples. Yes, they certainly should - and strive to avoid misbehaving in full view of impressionable youngsters who idolise them.

Many do indeed set good examples, in public at least. Rolf Harris certainly has for years. It's what some get up to out of the limelight that's often the issue.

But, as with radicalised political militants, flesh-biting footballers or anyone else found acting violently, criminally or in any way socially unacceptably, we must investigate the reasons why.

We have to return to the source, the cause of the trouble, and address it effectively enough to ensure those people don't repeat offend and others don't similarly foul up.

We as a society must shoulder at least some of the blame and not simply tut-tut, grab the pitchforks or blithely scapegoat those actually exposed as messed-up individuals.

Let's face it, we're all flipping messed up, one way or another in varying degrees, and to shout abuse, point our fingers then plunge our heads firmly back in the sand just sidesteps our shared responsibility to mould a better, nicer, wiser community.

Nothing changes, no improvements are made and problems remain unsolved.

Only he who is without sin can cast stones, people in glass houses shouldn't chuck missiles at neighbours, and those with dirty great planks in their own eyes have absolutely no right to point out the splinters in others'.

These three great sayings sort of sum up what I'm trying to express. Of course wrongdoers need to be dealt with and neutralised. Punishments should match the seriousness of bad behaviour.

Obviously being raped, beaten up or burgled is deeply distressing and very damaging – physically, mentally or both. I'm as keen as anyone to see an end to crime. I'm just saying that the best way to achieve this is to cut out its cancerous causes at root.

Of course we should all be protected from harm - especially children. But we shouldn't be too gung-ho, conceited or hypocritical about it. That's all.

**July 2** – Inspired by watching Glasto on telly, I went out today and bought second-hand copies of albums by Arcade Fire, Jake Bugg, Robert Plant and the Pixies on CD. I also got Calvin Harris, the Levellers, David Bowie, Rita Ora, Eric Clapton and Ocean Colour Scene. Oh yes!

**July 3** – Another birthday – this time it'd my adopted sister Suzette Glover's 63rd. I put some money in a card and posted it to her the other day. Hope she has a good one!

A new lyric started crystallizing in my mind as I watched Disclosure's Glastonbury set again on catch-up TV yesterday evening. This time, I started with the title and chorus and then did the verses. Here it is:

***Brain Freeze***

***Martin Money, July 2-3, 2014***

*Brain freeze, brain freeze yeah - you've got another nasty case of brain freeze*

*As they lock away a bad man that the nation idolised*
*And your thoughts are so damned tangled that your mind is paralysed*
*You've got another nasty case of brain freeze*

*As they balance their accounts by robbing cash from poor and sick*
*And you feel your skull's imploding 'coz they never miss a trick*

*When the cultures clash like crazy as the vultures swoop to feed*
*With their self-obsessed agendas based on envy, hate and greed*
*you've got another nasty case of brain freeze*

*Brain freeze, brain freeze yeah – you've got another nasty case of brain freeze*

*When the guilty get off lightly while the innocent are framed*
*And the vipers of the Press don't give a toss who's named and shamed*

*As they spread their dirty poison changing all the rules so fast*
*And the stars cascade in showers leaving followers aghast*
*You've got another nasty case of brain freeze.*

*If the crescent moon is twisted and the cross is upside down*
*As the mirror image shimmers it's a blood smeared circus clown*
*You've got another nasty case of brain freeze.*


Today's Thursday and I've been immersing myself in Glastonbury music all week via catch-up TV. I've now watched most of the televised sets, some of them twice.

**July 4** – Rolf Harris has been jailed for five years and nine months after being convicted of 12 indecent assaults on four girls – one of them just eight years old.

And former News of the World editor Andy Coulson faces 18 months behind bars for conspiring to hack phones. He was once David Cameron's communications director.
How the mighty are fallen!

**July 5** – It's my mate Carl's 50th birthday today. His partner Sam's laying on a surprise party for him with several of us at a new burger restaurant in Southbourne later on for a tea-time meal, followed by drinkies back at their house afterwards.

My birthday present to Carl was his ticket for the Gary Numan concert we attended together on Monday.  We met Jem there, and Carl hooked up with his mate Dave, who we've seen at all the local rock gigs we've been to since UFO in February 2013.

I'm playing Rita Ora's album, simply called Ora, as I type this. It's very good, and reinforces my view that there are some excellent female pop stars around right now.

Ellie Goulding and Paloma Faith have also joined Katy Perry, Lily Allen, Kate Nash, Lady Gaga, Adele and Pink in the ranks of great girl-power solo performers.

And of course Madonna and Kylie are still around, along with the evergreen Dolly Parton, Kate Bush, Joni Mitchell, Patti Smith, Stevie Nicks and Marianne Faithfull, to name just a few.

Keeping the flag flying for the fellers are new boys Jake Bugg, Tom Odell, John Newman, Passenger and Ed Sheeran, all set to take their places alongside the likes of Paul Weller, Robbie Williams, Neil Young, Paul McCartney, David Bowie, Elton John, Bob Dylan, Robert Plant and Stevie Wonder in the roll call of living male icons.

**July 6** – Yesterday provided another of life's good moments – or several, as it goes.

Carl's golden day was a triumph with a cast of quite a few. His mates, including gig-goer Dave, a guy called  Sam and his lady Sarah, joined Jem, Rich, Sonia, her son Ziggy, Jac, Bec, Alex, Charley, Russell, Sharon, Jimmy,  Sam Excell, Rudy, Bailey, Albert, Blaze and me for either the meal, the drinkies, or both.

Tina couldn't make it due t illness in her family.

The burger restaurant, called Quarters, has only been open a few weeks and I'd certainly go there again and recommend it to family and friends. My chicken burger was delicious and everyone praised the food.

Later, we went back to Sam and Carl's for a party. Luckily the rain held off so people were able to sit in the garden as well and not all cram into the house. A good day all round, I'd say. I just hope the birthday boy agrees. I asked him a couple of times if he was enjoying his day and he said yes.

Right! – I had a few cans of lager and some other odd concoctions at Carl's shindig. Now the question is do I go to the pub tonight?

I haven't been for a few weeks and I do miss it these days if I don't keep up regular attendances - thanks to Mark and Laura's success in making it a proper local again.

And yes, it will soon officially be called the Bell again. A special day marking this reversion has been arranged for Friday August 8 with a barbeque, bouncy castles, face-painting and so on. Great!

So do I go tonight? I should really knock the booze on the head till next weekend in light of yesterday's revelries that have left me a bit washed out and feeling icky.
I'll see how I am later then decide. In other words, play it by ear, like I tend to nowadays. Yesterday was a belter though, so either way, I'm happy!

**July 7** – I went to the Bell yesterday evening after all – and again I'm glad I did. I had a very pleasant time chatting to John Palmer and John Gaynor while listening to the amateur singers – Sunday night being karaoke night.

Matt Brandt, Dani Knight, Jenny Daniels and Tim Robbins were also there.

It's Ringo Starr's 74th birthday and the ninth anniversary of the London Bombs. I've lit a candle for the victims.

**July 9** – Brazil's high hopes of lifting the World Cup on home soil lie shattered in the dust this morning after a devastating 7-1 defeat by a rampant Germany in last night's semi-final.

The five times winners of the coveted trophy were torn to shreds and totally humiliated by a brilliant and clinically ruthless German side in one of the most shocking results in the tournament's history.

And, to further rub salt in the wounds, German striker Miroslav Klose overtook Brazil's revered Ronaldo to become the World Cup's all-time top scorer by netting his 16th goal while making his fourth appearance in the competition's finals.

Three times winners Germany emphatically booked their place in the final, where they will face either Holland or Argentina, who play each other later today.

The Brazilians, badly missing injured talisman striker Neymar and organising powerhouse skipper Silva – yellow-carded – were as abysmal as the Germans were impressive. The defending was shockingly poor for a match at such a high level.

As the football-mad host nation tries to come to terms with its most devastating defeat ever, German people are celebrating all the way to Sunday's final.

I don't much envy the Brazilian team, now forced to handle this crushing blow and regroup in time for Saturday's third-place play-off against today's losers.

**July 10** – Those losers are Holland – but only just. Yesterday's match was the total opposite of the 7-1 drubbing we'd watched the previous evening.

With the score standing at 0-0, it went into extra time, then penalties, which Argentina won 4-2 to secure their place in the final.

Unlike the Germany-Brazil tie, this was a quite dull match as two sides well aware of what was at stake played safe and cancelled each other out.

But it's been proven time and time again that being dull can win you trophies if you play well and take your chances when they arise, whereas being too swashbuckling can leave you wide open to counter-attack, failure and humiliation.

Sadly for us, football isn't always a spectator sport – even when the usually mesmerising Dutch are playing.

But their success in finishing at least fourth in the World Cup bodes well for Manchester United, due to be managed by the Dutch national coach Louis van Gaal when the new Premier League season kicks off next month.
So Holland now play Brazil on Saturday in the third-place play-off, and Argentina meet the Germans in Sunday's final.

All in all, it's been a great tournament for football fans with some dazzling performances and truly exciting matches packed with wonderful moments.

And England fans could watch most of it in relaxed mode – once our boys were out, we could sit back and enjoy the action and drama minus the butt-clenching tension.

Of course it's a great shame England didn't do better and we would have much preferred to endure the frayed nerves and bitten fingernails.  Roll on the Euros!

**********************************************

# CHAPTER SIX – ANGELS AND DEMONS

**July 11** – An old lyric of mine came back to me last night as I was watching the telly:

Well I know I ain't no angel – I've had my share of "fun"
But the Good Lord is my witness that I never fired that gun- no, no…
And I ain't killed nobody as my Maker has the proof
I said they got the wrong man but only God knows it's the truth.

Its part of a piece called Wrong Man Blues, which I wrote in June 1977. And it resurfaced in my mind as I caught the latest instalment of Coronation Street.

One of the soap's current storylines is about a feller called Michael, an ex-burglar just released from prison. He's being played surprisingly well by Les Dennis, better known as a comedian, TV presenter and game show host.

In last night's episode, Michael got upset and angry that everyone thought a costly wide screen TV he'd just given someone as a present was stolen. It wasn't – he bought it with money just received, left to him in a recently-deceased relative's will.

The lyric came back to me as I noticed a distinct parallel between this fictional TV tale and something I'd read in Pete Townsend's autobiography a few hours earlier.

Rock guitarist-songwriter Townsend was telling how he unwittingly and completely innocently became tangled up in an internet child porn scandal when he tried to help disadvantaged Russian orphans.

Both stories – one pure fantasy, the other painfully real for the unfortunate musician – brought home forcefully to me how dangerous and damaging suspicion and assumption can be.

Hypocrisy and a mob rule mentality take over as people become wrongly accused, ostracised and even assaulted by others far too quick to jump to conclusions, conveniently forgetting their own very real misdemeanours in the process.

And this applies whether you're blameless in the matter under consideration – like Townsend  – or an ex-con who's gone straight, trying to live a crime-free normal life, such as the soap character Michael. The stain is indelible, the stigma permanent.

Let he who is without sin, and all that.

In the final analysis, none of us is a complete angel and we all have our demons, large or small.  It's so easy to overlook this when we're sanctimoniously slating others.

I, for one, am ashamed, angry and appalled at myself for some of the ways I've treated certain people, especially family and friends. But we can't alter the past.

Instead, we have to make amends as best we can in whatever ways possible in order to produce good, positive vibrations cancelling out the bad.

Continuing on the television theme, there was a programme on later yesterday evening called Power to the People. It was on the Vintage TV music channel.

Filmed performances by Tom Robinson, Public Enemy, Frankie goes to Hollywood, Marvin Gaye, the Clash, the Manic Street Preachers, Pink Floyd, Edwin Starr and the Sex Pistols featured in the hour-long show.

Their songs bristled with indignation and rage, making me ask where oh where are the new champions of protest and social justice in our varied, interesting, occasionally brilliant but actually pretty safe and harmless pop landscape?

There's certainly enough to get steamed up about with the state of the world in general and our coalition government's savage, unfair policies.

Sure, some pop, rock and rap stars still deliberately say and do things to shock, but there's no real point, depth or social conscience in their words or actions.

I think we're well overdue another incisive movement like early rock, punk, reggae or rap to stir things up, confront people and shake them out of their apathetic stupor.

**July 14** – History's been made with Germany's triumph in the World Cup Final. They beat Argentina 1-0 to become the first European team to lift the trophy on South American soil.

It's the fourth time the Germans have won the tournament, matching Italy's achievement. Brazil have five to their name, Uruguay and Argentina two apiece and France, Spain and England each have one.

With the score level at 0-0, the match went into extra time, with rising new German star Gotze finding the net with 113 minutes played.

So with that excitement behind us now we look forward to the new football season starting next month.   Come on Slough Town, AFC Bournemouth, Manchester United and England as we bid to qualify for the 2016 Euros.

**July 15** – There's been a cabinet reshuffle in the coalition government.  What effect it will have on us as a nation only time will tell, but there are now more women and Euro-sceptics in the ranks.

Philip Hammond replaces William Hague as Foreign Secretary, with Hague staying on in the cabinet as Leader of the Commons.

Several men have gone in the shake-up, including veteran Ken Clarke who is standing down.

The 74-year-old has had a high-profile career during which he's been Home Secretary, Chancellor of the Exchequer and held various other top jobs in successive Tory governments.

Environment Secretary Owen Paterson is being replaced by education minister Liz Truss. And Nicky Morgan is Education Secretary, taking over from Michael Gove.

**July 16** – Happy birthday to my great mate Kerry Smith, and also to our mutual friend Kelly Millen.  Hope they both have good ones!

**July 17** – And today it's the turn of Jen Wheeler, former barmaid at the Bell. Her affectionate nickname at the time was

"Dotty." But on a sadder note, we've heard that inspirational blues guitar legend Johnny Winter has died aged 70.

**July 18** – The international news is dominated by a plane crash with a difference. Malicious intent is strongly suspected after nearly 300 people perished as a Malaysian
Airlines jet plunged to Earth over eastern Ukraine yesterday.

Everyone on board the Boeing 777 is presumed dead after the incident that scattered debris over a wide area close to the Russian border.

Flight MH17 from Amsterdam to Kuala Lumpur was travelling over the conflict-hit region when it disappeared from radar. It was carrying 283 passengers and 15 crew.

Most were Dutch, many were Australian, but the victims were of various nationalities, including nine Brits.

As the world comes to terms with this shocking event, there are sensational claims that Ukrainian rebels, backed by Russia, deliberately shot down the aircraft.

But as an urgent investigation into the crash is launched, one burning question needs to be answered – whether this was a tragic accident or a terrorist act, why oh why was this plane being flown so dangerously close to a known war zone?

About 100 of its passengers were thought to be bound for an international AIDS and HIV conference in Australia.

Angry Tony Abbott, Australia's prime minister, has blasted Russia's response to what he sees as a crime against humanity.

Russian president Vladimir Putin merely blamed Ukraine and washed his hands of any responsibility for the volatile situation in that high-risk region.

Abbott warned Putin not to hamper the investigation but to co-operate fully.

Other world leaders, including US president Barack Obama, Dutch Prime Minister Mark Rutte, Germany's Angela Merkel and our Prime Minister David Cameron have also expressed their shock and alarm.

It's the second major incident involving Malaysian Airlines this year – on March 8; a similar plane owned by the same company vanished without trace an hour after taking off from Kuala Lumpur. It's yet to be found.

Meanwhile, in other news, the Israelis and Palestinians continue their lethal tit-for-tat fire fight over the Gaza strip.

**July 20** – Remembering my mate Umo, who passed over three years ago today. Doesn't seem that long. I've put a tribute on Facebook and lit a candle for him.

Umo was an amiable, likeable and popular guy, well known in local pubs. We used to have quite lengthy, interesting and animated chats about all sorts of things including Manchester United, music, motorbikes … and Cornish pasties. RIP buddy.

**July 21** – Comedy fans had a real treat on TV last night when Gold showed the final reunion show of the legendary and highly influential Monty Python.

Comparisons with the Beatles and the Goons were inevitable as comedy giants such as Steve Coogan, Mike Myers and Eddie

Izzard paid glowing tribute to the men who inspired them. Scientists Brian Cox and Stephen Hawking also joined in the fun.

The half live, half film clip show paid fitting tribute to Graham Chapman, the only Python unable to physically be there due to his sad, untimely death in 1989.

And it was an absolute joy to see John Cleese, Terry Jones, Eric Idle, Michael Palin and Terry Gilliam on stage together re-running some of their most famous sketches.

The kings of surreal comedy were back in town – and, although older, greyer and less agile, still able to make us laugh at their brilliant treatment of life's absurdities.

To guys of my age, the influence of Monty Python cannot be over-stated. It's a case of you had to be there to appreciate the massive, far-reaching impact they had.

Needless to say, I loved watching it all on television. But my mates Carl and Jem both went up to London the day before – Saturday – to see the show in the flesh at the O2 Arena.

Our mutual friend Sharon bought their tickets as 50th birthday presents. Carl's golden day was a couple of weeks ago and Jem's is in August. Both are massive Python fans like me. Talk about cool gifts!

The Python show was a TV treat for me. But it was a different story earlier in the day, when I had the misfortune to watch a telly advert that really annoyed me.

Oh come on Money, you're probably thinking, you're going to have to narrow it down a bit – most TV commercials irritate you. True, but some more so than others.

The main reason this one got my goat so much was it portrayed a group of kids on a route march through woods, impersonating soldiers singing one of those mind-numbing call-and response songs said to enhance team-building. (Yeah, right!).

You know the ones – the leader sings a daft, infuriatingly banal phrase and then the following group sings it back to them in unison like a bunch of brainless mimics.

I get just as steamed up over that dreadful work-placed pensions "we're all in" commercial - because that, too, shows human beings as sheep-like creatures incapable of independent thought and needing someone to lead them by the nose at all times.

It's the kind of mindset some organisations are built upon – especially military ones. Significantly, in many cases, the nauseatingly obedient flock dress in matching clothing. Individuality is stifled. Mob rule prevails. And that's very, very scary.

Okay, granted, we all need a certain degree of structure, organisation, boundaries, rules and guidelines in our dealings with each other. The alternative is to have anarchy and chaos.

I fully accept that in some cases, having immediately-identifiable uniforms is important – police officers, fire fighters, nurses, lifeguards and suchlike.

And military groups obviously need strong, decisive leadership and a keen sense of discipline - otherwise they're ineffective.

But I've never seen the logic or the need for so many commercial businesses to enforce such strict dress codes – except in the hospitality and service industries where people need to easily spot an air steward, waitress or hotel porter when they need to.

And I've always opposed the idea of school uniforms, seeing them as inextricably linked into a cold, brutal system intent on kicking kids into line, controlling and indoctrinating them at every turn from an early age. Just another brick in the wall.

I find it worrying that something as apparently innocuous but insidious and highly influential as a TV ad break can be used with increasing regularity to feed us such sinister messages – in this case, fall meekly into line and follow us; don't try to think because we know best!

Before leaving the subject of TV adverts I must register my disgust and dismay at the one featuring a huge pigeon crapping pink goo on people, currently being shown blatantly in the daytime when highly impressionable kids will be watching. Ye gods!

Right – mini-rant over.

On a sad note, legendary James Garner, one of the first actors to be successful in both film and television, has died at the age of 86.

One of his most famous roles was in the star-studded classic war film The Great Escape but my first recollection of seeing him was in the lead role of Maverick in the groundbreaking US comedy western series on black and white telly when I was a boy.

Like many, I especially enjoyed watching him as Jim Rockford in the clever, humorous and original American detective series The Rockford files in the 1970s.

It was a fore-runner of great modern programmes mixing crime and comedy like our own New Tricks – cracking stories, well presented and told with wit and great style.

**July 23** - As widely suspected, it's now been confirmed – Peaches Geldof died of a heroin overdose.  A coroner decided this earlier today after hearing evidence at the resumed inquest.

It would be a tragic death anyway, but it just seems especially sad when such incidents involve people that young – 25 – talented and popular.

Poor Peaches will never reach 30, let alone 40 or 50.

In sharp contrast, my pal Russell Hall – Sam's ex, Becca and Alex's dad – celebrated his golden birthday yesterday.  Happy birthday mate!

The controversy over the downed passenger plane rumbles on as we await the start of the Commonwealth Games this evening, when host city Glasgow stages the opening ceremony. We wish all our athletes the very best.

A more humorous news item involves a tree honouring George Harrison.  Planted in his memory in a Los Angeles park in 2004, it's died after being infested by ...beetles!

Oh the irony!  No doubt George and his great buddy John Lennon are having a good old chuckle together about this in the afterlife.

**July 25** – England had a great first day at the Commonwealth Games, ending up top of the medals table with 17, including six golds.  Australia is currently second with 15 medals, Scotland third with 10, India fourth with seven and Canada fifth with four.

Scotland, the host nation, has four golds so far, including two for the same family.  Kimberley Renicks and her sister Louise each won their events in the judo.

There's more talk on the news today about a so-called economic recovery.  I remain deeply sceptical.

With next year's general election edging ever closer, the coalition carve-up merchants seem to be getting more and more desperate to convince us that their dreadful, disastrous policies are actually working.

Well they might be able to fool themselves, cosseted in their fantasy world of political spin, number crunching and grand economic theories.  But no-one I know sees an improvement – quite the opposite.

Companies are still going bust – like my publishers – and people are still losing their jobs, such as a couple of mates of mine who recently finally managed to find work after ages of looking, only to be laid off again within weeks!

And I've yet to meet anyone actually prospering in this alleged economic revival – most people are struggling to get by, decidedly worse off than they were before this awful bunch got into power.

I have a horrible feeling Cameron and Co will actually succeed in persuading enough voters things are on the up again to get back into Downing Street, paving the way for more cuts and cruelty.

Even if the outrageous revival claim was true, I'd still say it's hardly a success story with so much lasting damage being done to millions of citizens' lives along the way.

**July 26** – Just had a fab few hours with the family.  Phil and Emily came over with Chloe and we all went down Southbourne seafront in the blazing sunshine.

Chloe thoroughly enjoyed her first experience of a sandy beach and paddling in the sea with her dad's help.

We also had an ice cream from a cliff top kiosk on our way down to the prom and ended with refreshing pints of cool lager shandy in the pub on the way back to the car.

Magic moments!

Now I'm off to a burger bar to celebrate Russell's 50th the other day and Sam's birthday on Monday (today being a Saturday).

**July 27** – Yep – all in all, yesterday was a very good one for me.  After the family beach adventure, I came home for a while to change my sweaty clothes and chill for a few minutes before meeting up with Russell, Sam, Carl, Jem and other friends for the burger meal followed by drinkies back at Sam's.

**August 4** – The Commonwealth Games have drawn to a close in Glasgow with England topping the medals table. Our boys and girls excelled themselves, winning 174 in all, 58 of them gold.  Runners-up Australia got 137, Canada got 82 and Scotland came fourth with 53.

Fifth-placed India actually won more medals than the host nation – 64 in all – but fewer golds. So with the top prizes total taking preference, Scotland clinched it. Wales came 13th with 36 medals and Northern Ireland 15th (with 12).

It's so nice to see England triumphing as a nation rather than its athletes being lumped together with others from neighbouring countries under some pointless Team GB banner, as in the Olympics.

Several new sporting stars emerged from the Games, boding well for the home nations. And the event itself has been hailed as an outstanding success.

Meanwhile, in my own little corner of existence, it looks like I've sorted out a new publisher so Volume Seven (Persistent Illusions) will be out before too long. Volumes One to Six will also be back in circulation soon with little extra expense. Cool!

Which leaves this volume, number eight, nearing completion. With England's successes at the Commonwealth Games, my books about to be back in the public domain, landmark birthdays all over the place and rock gigs and mini-break excursions to look forward to, I'm finishing it on a high.

And in a symbolic and very welcome move, my beloved local pub is being officially re-launched on Friday, reverting back from Seabourne's Bar - it's daft name for the past five years - to the Bell (hooray!). So it's all good.

Sure, there's still plenty of bad stuff around. Today is the 100th anniversary of the outbreak of World War One - and it's being marked with numerous special occasions.

Death and destruction, conflict, hatred, division, tragedy and misery are all still with us.  But so are rays of hope and more pleasant aspects of living on this mad planet.  And it's these I'd point to as I prepare to end this section of my journal.

******************************************

# CHAPTER SEVEN – SHARED MISSION

I've called this book Patience and Wisdom – partly to give it a pleasant, positive feel and partly to emphasize the importance of both qualities in the modern world.

How we desperately need them in our dealings with each other and the rest of creation. But we also require compassion, tolerance, understanding, acceptance, respect and forgiveness.

In fact, all are present in much larger measures than a cursory glance at the newspapers or TV news might suggest.

Amid all the wars, disasters, pain and misery there are actually plenty of good acts and stories to be found – if only we look hard enough.

We have to enhance and add to these in a big way if we're to succeed in improving things for everyone's benefit.

It's not all doom and gloom – honest – but it could and should be a heck of a lot better.  We just have to try harder to disperse the dark energy and promote the light.

That is our shared mission, brothers and sisters.  Up for it?

Till the next time then.  Tatty bye and take care…

**Spread the love, live in peace - Martin Money, August 4, 2014.**

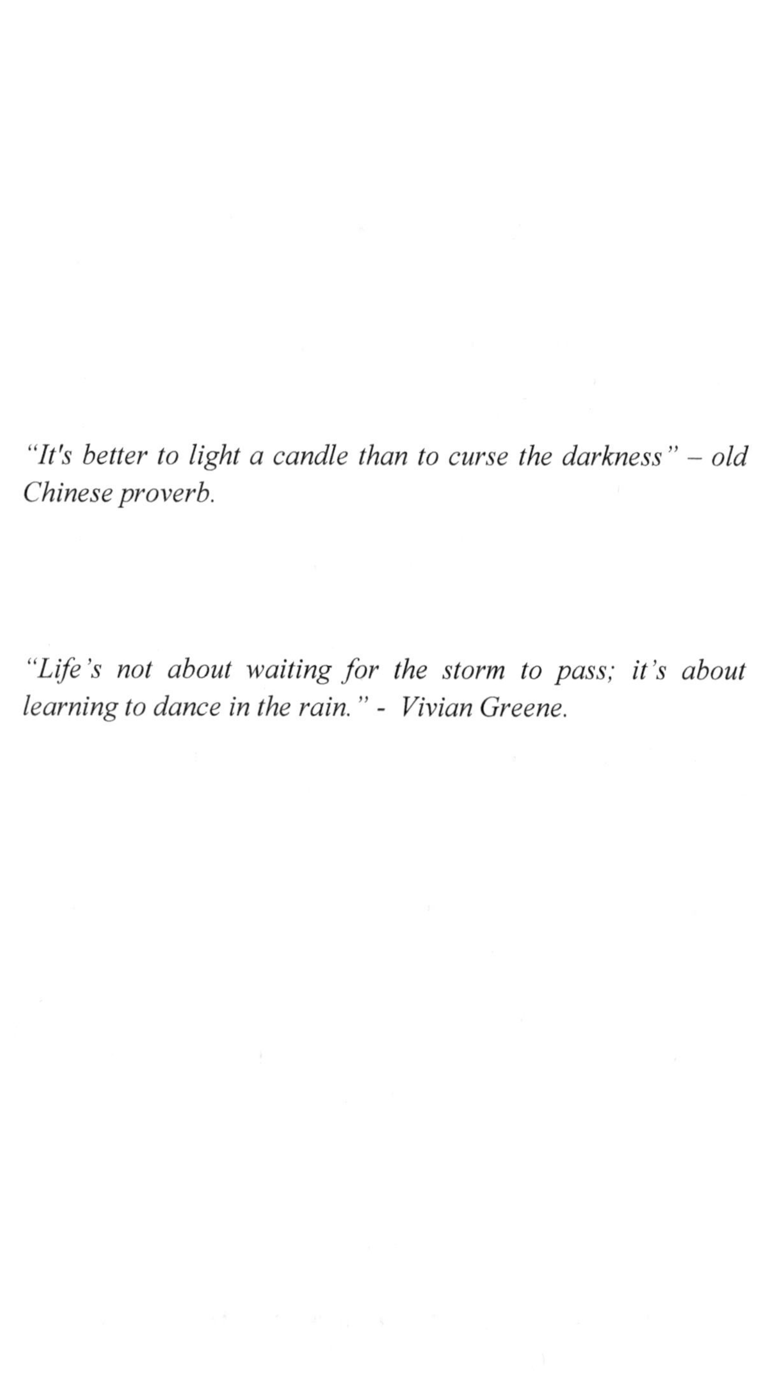

*"It's better to light a candle than to curse the darkness" – old Chinese proverb.*

*"Life's not about waiting for the storm to pass; it's about learning to dance in the rain." - Vivian Greene.*

This book is dedicated to the memory of Stephen Sutton, an amazing and truly inspirational young man who used the last four years of a life cut tragically short by illness to raise millions of pounds for cancer sufferers while inspiring others to face hardship with good grace, dignity and a smile.

It is further written in honour of my amazing family and friends – indeed, everyone who's touched my life with companionship, compassion, humour and joy.

And all carriers of the positive vibration through the ages - the truth tellers, wisdom imparters, harmony bringers and enlightened healers. Much respect!


**One Love peeps, One Love – M. M.**

Born in Slough on February 25, 1954, Martin Money lived there until early adulthood, moving to Dorset in 1978.

Leaving school with three A levels and seven O levels, he worked in a bank for a few months before starting a 24-year career in regional newspaper journalism that ended in redundancy in 1997.

Since then he's had a variety of part-time jobs and also worked as a volunteer for charities.

A proud father and grandfather, he lives in Bournemouth where he enjoys short cliff top walks, writing, reading, watching TV and socialising.

*Author's photo by Sam Excell*